The Insightful Reader

How to Learn Deeply & Attain Life-Changing Insights from Books

By I. C. Robledo

https://mentalmax.net/AMZbks

The Insightful Reader: How to Learn Deeply & Attain Life-Changing Insights from Books

Disclaimer

Although the author and publisher have made every effort to ensure that the information in this book was correct at press time, the author and publisher do not assume and hereby disclaim any liability to any party for any loss, damage, or disruption caused by errors or omissions, whether such errors or omissions result from negligence, accident, or any other cause.

This book is not intended as a substitute for the medical advice of physicians. The reader should regularly consult a physician in matters relating to his/her health and particularly with respect to any symptoms that may require diagnosis or medical attention.

The views expressed are those of the author alone and should not be taken as expert instruction or commands. The reader is responsible for his or her own actions.

Adherence to all applicable laws and regulations, including international, federal, state, and local governing professional licensing, business practices, advertising, and all other aspects of doing business in the US, Canada, or any other jurisdiction is the sole responsibility of the purchaser or reader.

Neither the author nor the publisher assumes any responsibility or liability whatsoever on the behalf of the purchaser or reader of these materials.

Any perceived slight of any individual or organization is purely unintentional.

Table of Contents

An Introduction

The Best Time to Be a Reader

As of 2020, around 150 million books exist – and thousands more are being published every day. Clearly, we have an abundance of books to choose from. We also have many different ways that we can read, as regardless of how you prefer to do so, there will be a format to suit your preference. There are paperback books, digital books (i.e., eBooks), audiobooks, libraries, book subscription services, summarized versions of books, literary analyses, free books online (e.g., Gutenberg.org), and even braille and large-print books. This means that for any book you want to read, you will likely be able to find and read it however you like.

The main downside today is that there are far too many books to read in a lifetime, and so we must take some time to find the right books for us. But, realize that this is a silly downside – it is as if saying the issue with having an abundance of food is that there is too much to eat in a lifetime. The task of the modern human is to adjust to overabundance – to learn to find the right books for us, rather than to become overwhelmed with the selection and avoid reading altogether. Ultimately, we must learn to choose the great books that are most worth reading for our purposes and learn to read them well.

Imagine what it would have been like to be alive 500 years ago. Let's suppose that you were an apprentice, starting out in your career and you were expected to focus your time on developing *one* skill or trade until you mastered it, and then you could have your own apprentices work under you. For the most part, people were not literate and so this would have been your most viable option – to specialize in one ability and perform or instruct in that skill for the rest of your life. In the present day, of course, reading is something that is accessible to virtually all of us. This means that we are now in the position to develop as many skills as we wish, and to learn as much about any number of topics as we wish. We are free to explore, not tied down to one domain for life as we would have been 500 years ago.

If we know how to read effectively, we hold the power to improve ourselves, help others to improve, and meet our true purpose and goals in life. Most importantly, with reading we will be unlimited in our capacity for learning. Unlike our ancestors from centuries ago, we are always capable of learning in a wide range of new topics. Our potential back then was quite limited, yet today we are limitless. There is nothing stopping us now.

Goals of *The Insightful Reader*

Choose the right books to read

Finding the right books is not always easy, but it is worth taking some time to look for them. Some people get lost at this stage and give up on reading before they even start. This is understandable, as it can seem overwhelming to find books that you like or which you can benefit from when there are so many to choose from. But with practice, it is not so difficult to find some books that you will enjoy or that will be useful to you. To get you started, I have provided many book recommendations throughout *The Insightful Reader* for you to check out. I have also included a *Recommended Readings* section of over 200 books, for you to have all of my book recommendations in one convenient place. These will provide a starting point to help you choose valuable and insightful books to read.

Get more out of what you read

The modern world bombards us with information. It is pervasive, and more and more is being generated every day, to a level where we must learn to sift through it all and make sense of it more efficiently. Much of this information is available to us in written form. Thus, the world demands that we be high quality readers and thinkers, and that we be able to skillfully apply the knowledge we acquire. Many of us will read for work or to meet a specific need or goal. This means we must master the most important reading strategies and skills to make the greatest possible progress in our lives.

In reality, many of us have bad reading habits, such as we may not make any time to read on a regular basis. Or we may read passively, not asking questions about the book we are reading. We may read material where we already know most of the information, rather than seeking out material where we can actually learn something new. Most of us make some mistakes in our approaches to reading. The good news is that most of the mistakes we tend to make can be fixed with the tips given in *The Insightful Reader*.

In this book, I will aim to provide you with general principles that can be applied to your specific reading goals and objectives. You will find that often there is no hard and fast rule that will apply for everyone in every case. In fact, you will need to read this book actively with your full mental energy to figure out how you can best apply it to meet your needs. This will be the case with most books you read. Be aware that if you are falling asleep while reading, you will not gain much from the experience. I need you to sit up and stay wide awake on this reading journey. You should be an active participant.

Create a better, richer life for yourself through reading

It is paramount that we use reading to improve ourselves. In improving ourselves, we will be in a better position to help others improve, and then to help improve the status of the world. To begin, we should think about what is lacking in our lives, what we are unhappy with, what we can improve, and then read books that help us to move forward in a positive direction. To do this fruitfully, we will need to apply the principles we learn from the books we read and put them into action. We do not always need to read with the specific objective to improve our lives or the lives of others, but this is important enough that we should keep it in mind when we choose our next book. There is no single type of reading that is required for this. You can make progress through reading many different types of books: self-development, philosophy, business, science, history, literature, or in other areas.

Become an *Insightful Reader*

Overall, the focus here will be to help you choose the best books to read, to get the most from them, and to live a richer life through your readings. We will examine systems to go deeper into a book, which often involve reading more deliberately and thoughtfully, and taking notes along the way, for those who want to obtain the greatest benefits from a highly valuable book. Also, we will cover more speedy systems that involve scanning, skimming, and flipping through parts of a book, in aims to get to the parts that truly matter for you. In the end, you will find that the best reader is an **Insightful Reader** – which is *someone who knows how to read with the purpose of seeking out valuable insights and a deep understanding.*

Cultivate a passion for reading

I am truly passionate about books and reading and I hope that this shines through in this book and rubs off on you and motivates you to read more books, think about the books you read, take more notes on them, discuss what you read with friends and family, and ultimately be happier and more fulfilled with what you are reading. Those who are passionate, excited, or at least interested in reading are the ones who will ultimately gain the most from the books that they read, including this one.

Who am I and What do I Know About Reading?

I would like to tell you briefly about my background and qualifications for writing this book. I have my master's degree in industrial-organizational psychology, and I have written 12 books in self-development and mind-brain improvement. One of my most popular titles in self-development is ***7 Thoughts to Live Your Life By: A Guide to the Happy, Peaceful, & Meaningful Life***, which I recommend reading after you have finished this book.

Since I was a child, I remember getting an immense joy from reading. I was lucky enough to have parents who instilled the habit of reading in me at an early age – teaching me to read in English *and* Spanish. In those early years, I recall often wanting to read a book, and my parents made sure to provide a supportive environment for this. There was always a great selection of books that I could read from. In my later childhood and early adulthood, I focused more on reading books for school during the school year, and I read more books of my own choosing during the summers.

After I earned my master's degree and finished my formal education, I decided that *I should read more*, since I was no longer required to read anything for school. I realized that I was free to read anything I wished, and that I could direct my mind toward learning more about anything at all. Since then I have read about 40 books per year in a wide variety of topics. At the point of this book's publication, I have read about 400 books, and I have detailed notes on the most important 40 books I have read. I have also read thousands of news, entertainment, and blog articles, hundreds of academic articles, and hundreds of short stories and poems.

Reading is important to me because I want to know all that I can know, understand all that I can, and I want to learn from the greatest minds who have put their words on paper. I am very curious, especially about the big questions in life, many of which do not seem to have definitive answers. Ultimately, I believe that reading is the most efficient and lowest-cost way to learn, which is why I am a tremendous fan of this form of learning.

If your background is nothing like mine and you feel that you did not grow up in such a supportive environment for reading – perhaps your family did not read much, and you did not grow up with many books or much natural interest in them – there is no need to worry. The fact that you are reading this now shows that you are interested in becoming a better reader and developing your reading skills, and that is an excellent first step. I will do my best to teach you some of the skills I have learned which have been hugely valuable in my reading journey. Some of these came naturally to me, and some were learned through trial and error in my constant efforts to improve my reading abilities. Do not feel that you need to be a natural or expert reader to make good use of this book – I have especially written *The Insightful Reader* assuming that you have a lot of room to grow, as we all do. Whether you are beginning your reading journey, or even if you consider yourself an expert reader, you will find some nuggets of wisdom here that can help take your reading to a higher level. You may even spot some major flaws in your reading patterns that you can begin to rectify.

I am aware that there are many people who have read much more and much faster than me, but I have thought critically and deeply about how we can *choose the best books to read*, *improve our reading abilities,* and *get the most value from the books we read*, which is not something that most readers do. Many of us simply employ the same habits over and over from when we learned to read as children. Thus, I think the advice in this book will be especially useful for someone who wants to improve his reading abilities, and who is open to reexamining his reading processes in efforts to improve them.

Now, I would like you to consider what your personal reading goal is. How much do you wish to read, and what do you wish to gain from your readings? My personal goal is to read a thousand insightful books in my lifetime and to understand them deeply rather than just superficially, and to be highly knowledgeable in many fields such as psychology, philosophy, business, history, and the sciences. Whether your goal is similar to mine or not, I believe this book will be a useful tool to help you meet your reading goals.

Before You Continue . . .

As a thank you for reading, I want you to have a free guide called:

Step Up Your Learning: Free Tools to Learn Almost Anything

Have you ever wondered what the best sites and resources for learning are? It takes time and effort to figure out which sites are worth it and which are not. I hope to save you some of that time so you can spend more of it learning instead of searching the Internet.

In the past ten years or so, there has been a free learning revolution happening. More and more resources for learning are becoming available to the public at no cost. With so many new ones coming out, it's easy to miss out on some of the great learning opportunities available. Fortunately for you, this guide is short at around 4,000 words, and tells you exactly what you need to know.

The guide stems from my own experiences of using a variety of learning sites and resources. In it, you will discover the best places to go for learning at no cost. Also, I'll explain which resources are best for you, depending on your learning goals.

You can download this free guide as a PDF by typing this website into your browser: http://mentalmax.net/EN

Now, let's get back on topic.

The Benefits of Reading

An Introduction

Just as I was beginning to work on writing *The Insightful Reader*, my mother called to tell me that my grandfather (e.g., my father's father) had passed away. Although he likely would not have imagined this, he was an inspirational figure behind this book.

When I was four years old, I once asked him to read me a book, as any child might ask his grandfather. With a slightly embarrassed look, he told me that he could not read. This was obviously a joke, and so I persisted in asking him to read to me. This time, my grandfather emphasized that it was not possible – he never learned to read. I was shocked – as a young child I had assumed that all adults could read. However, my grandfather did not grow up anything like I did – he had a much tougher life in a *rancho* (i.e., a very small and poor town) in Mexico where not knowing how to read was the norm. Survival, work, and caring for family were the priorities, not education. Paradoxically, through lacking the ability to read, my grandfather actually knew all too well the benefits of this ability. As a skilled and hard-working laborer, on many occasions he was offered promotions into management. Of course, he was happy to have his efforts recognized, but he always had to turn these opportunities down, as he understood that knowing how to read and write would be a requirement. The value of being literate was clear to him in these moments. He understood that books could be a portal into a better way of life, despite never having had the opportunity to learn to read himself.

In this section we will consider the many benefits that reading provides us with, and *how* it is that books can present us with a portal into a better way of life.

An Efficient Way to Learn

Generally, when we want to learn a vast amount of information, we have three main options. There is learning through reading, audio, or video formats. With reading, you only have access to words and sometimes diagrams or charts. With audio, you have spoken words and you can also gauge the emotional quality of those words. Through video, you have spoken words, the emotional quality is there, as well as a visual medium to help you understand the information.

With many options for learning, why should we focus on reading?

First, reading typically occurs at a faster rate than listening happens, often at about twice the speed. For example, the average reading speed is 200-400 words per minute, and the average speed of an audiobook or professional speaker is around 150 words per minute. This means that if you have the choice to listen to an audiobook or lecture, or instead to read a transcript or written book file assuming it is available, then you should choose the format that you can read visually. This will be more efficient than the alternative, generally. Of course, if you are able to listen to your content at a time or in a setting where you normally would not read, such as on a commute or while you are driving, then listening to the audio version will make perfect sense.

Another benefit of traditional reading (i.e., visually) is that you may have greater control over the speed of processing than if you are listening to a speech or to audio content. It is much easier to skip unimportant information, to slow down for more important parts, or to review something you did not understand when you are reading traditionally as opposed to with an audiobook. And if you are listening to a speaker, of course, you may not feel comfortable asking him to speed up, skip something, slow down, or repeat something – as this will probably not be appropriate.

To be clear, I do not recommend against using auditory or video forms of learning. In fact, I think any kind of reading or learning is beneficial. Although visual reading is normally more efficient, there are some cases when audiobooks can be an especially useful option for learning. For example, audiobooks can be an asset when there is a novel that you want to savor, rather than speed through. Perhaps you have even found a narrator who helps make the story spring to life.

Another reason to consider audiobooks more carefully is if you feel that you are much better at processing auditory information. Even if this is the case, not all information is available in audio, so it will still be valuable for you to continue practicing your traditional reading skills. As another example, perhaps you would like to learn a foreign language. If so, you may pursue audio formats to make sure that you are building your listening comprehension abilities rather than just your visual reading abilities. Keep in mind that if you still prefer to learn mostly in audio format, you may choose to speed up a recording to go 1.5 or 2 times the normal speed, to make it roughly as efficient as if you were reading the material normally. With some practice, you will be able to listen and understand most of the information even at this speed.

As to learning via video formats, this suffers from the same problem as audio content, because you can only absorb the information as fast as you can listen to it. And again, for most people this speed will be much slower than your visual reading speed. However, for someone who is struggling to understand a topic, watching videos that help to visualize and animate ideas could be helpful. On the other hand, for someone who does not need this, these features may just slow down the pace of learning. Again, when we read, we tend to absorb the information much faster. Also, with videos, you are not required to think carefully about how you can visualize the information yourself, because it is already done for you. Reading is more challenging because it requires more thought, imagination, reflection, and effort on your part, but in the end, this is better for your learning.

A critical point that makes visual reading superior for me is that when I read, there is silence. There are gaps of nothingness if I simply look away from the page. Silence comes at a great value to me. I find that when I want to truly learn and understand something, especially if it is a difficult or complex topic, I need some empty spaces to mentally digest the material. Rather, when you consume audio or visual content, the medium is unlikely to provide you with natural breaks for thinking. Of course, you can always pause the content to think, but few people will actually do this. Whereas with a book, when you arrive at the end of a page, of a section, or of a chapter, you may naturally stop and think about what it was that you just read. Silence promotes the act of thinking, as there is not a continuous stream of information coming in that you feel compelled to pay attention to.

If you want to attain the highest efficiency in your learning, the best format to read your books will be in paper. Meta-analytic studies have found that there is a statistically significant difference between reading in print versus reading on screens – print is slightly better. Personally, I aim to read more books in print, but of course eBooks or reading digitally is often much more convenient and cheaper. For more challenging reads, I prefer them in paper, and for lighter reads, I will sometimes read them in eBook or audiobook form. If you can only find a book in one format, of course, just read it that way, as long as this does not present you with any problems.

There are clearly other ways to learn beyond reading, audio, and video content. For example, there is learning through personal experience, which I believe is highly valuable and often necessary for learning physical skills. Traveling is an excellent way to learn about the world if you have the opportunity to do so. Of course, classes or lectures can be quite useful for learning as well. Games and apps can also be entertaining and socially engaging ways to learn about different topics, to help keep things interesting and stimulating. Despite the many wonderful tools for learning available, I believe that for most purposes, reading should be the primary way to learn, and other ways of learning can be used as a complement. Spend more time reading, and your level of understanding will grow much faster than with the alternatives. The reason it is not always as popular as other modes of learning is that it requires more effort and thought than most of the other vehicles for learning. Interestingly, it is this extra effort and thought required which likely creates a more fruitful learning experience.

A Low-Cost Way to Learn

In the movie *Goodwill Hunting*, Will (Matt Damon's character) tells a Harvard student "You dropped a hundred and fifty grand on an education you coulda got for a dollar fifty in late charges at the public library." Obviously, there is value in higher education, but Will implies that when you go to university, most of the value is being derived from books, and books can be accessed for free in libraries even if they have been written by experts who earned advanced degrees, and who themselves paid large sums of money in order to acquire that education. In essence, as long as you have strong reading abilities, self-discipline, and the ability to pick useful books to read for your purposes, you could acquire a great education at a very low cost (without earning a formal degree, of course).

You could either attain your education for free at the library, or you could even buy your books at full price and still the cost would not even approach that of a university degree. If you lament not having the means to pursue a college education, I would urge you to consider creating your own curriculum and becoming educated on your own terms. Allow your curiosity to guide your path. If you struggle to find a specific book through your library, simply ask your librarian for assistance – she may be able to get you an interlibrary loan or have some advice to help you access the book you desire. Actually, if you have any other questions about finding a similar book, or doing research on a topic, librarians generally have a wealth of helpful information. Do not be afraid to ask.

It is also possible to purchase courses or to attend an event to hear an expert give a talk. These can be useful ways to learn but consider that a course can cost hundreds or thousands of dollars and attending events can also be quite expensive. Often enough, these course developers or speakers will have published books which are available at a tiny fraction of those costs. And even if they have not, someone else will have written books on the topic that interests you. Personally, I tend to either read books to learn something, or hire an expert that I need to do a specific job for me if I find that this would be a more efficient use of my time (rather than learning how to do it myself). I generally do not find it worthwhile to pay for a course, especially if it seems that all of the material could easily have been stated or found in book format. I believe a key reason people pursue speakers or courses is that they expect the information to be more easily digestible. However, *something that is easily learned is also often easily forgotten*. It is not a bad thing to struggle through your learning process, which is called *effortful learning*. These are concepts I learned about in *Make it Stick* by Peter C. Brown, an excellent book on how to become a better learner.

If you lack funds to purchase many books, consider that an often-overlooked way to gain access to free books is to become a book reviewer. Many authors will feel uncomfortable if you email them asking for a free book, but if you ask for a review copy (these usually come in the form of a free PDF file), you may be surprised to find that you are much more likely to receive a favorable response. If you like the idea of reviewing books, you may even pursue different services that help reviewers find new books to review, such as NetGalley. However, I do not recommend signing up unless you truly look forward to reading new books and providing your helpful review when you finish.

Despite the many low cost or even free ways that exist to access books, I prefer to invest in my learning and in books. We tend to spend money on trivial things without much thought, yet with books people may complain that they are too expensive. Rather, we should keep in mind that the information in these books will ultimately contain much more value for you, contributing to your deep understanding of the world and of topics important to you. If you have the funds for it, I would urge you to purchase some books that will be important for your needs. For the most important books I read, I like having easy access to them in print, so that I can read through them whenever I wish.

Learn from Success Stories in History

Many people will attempt to succeed by following a hunch, through trial and error, or perhaps through seeking guidance from a colleague or employer. But doesn't it make more sense to learn from the collective successes of people throughout history? If you want to learn about what contributed to the success of Bill Gates, Sam Walton (i.e., Walmart founder), or Warren Buffett (i.e., one of the most successful investors of all time), you do not need a personal meeting with these people – which unless you are a personal contact, you would be highly unlikely to get anyway. What would be most beneficial is reading books that discuss their lives and how they accomplished what they did. If you value their personal input, you can even seek out the books that they have written or been interviewed for. Keep in mind that for anything you want to accomplish, someone has attempted this and succeeded at it in the past and you can *learn how* through books. Of course, you should learn about the topics that interest you, but it also helps to learn about how people have succeeded in your field. For example: what type of skills do you need, what challenges are you likely to face, and how can you handle the tough problems that are most likely to arise?

The most obvious caveat to reading about others' successes is that the world we live in is changing so fast that what contributed to past successes may not apply to you. For example, part of what allowed people to succeed in the past may have been that there was much less competition in those times (as population sizes were much smaller the farther you go back in history). Or a greater part than we realize may have simply been due to luck. However, even with such caveats, learning about great achievements through history is still worthwhile. We must simply focus on principles that are more likely to stand the test of time. You may find that through reading such books, you acquire unique knowledge and also an advantage over your competition. Reading about successes and people from different time periods will also provide you with a wider perspective, aiding you to keep in mind what is truly important instead of getting distracted with every new fad that is trending in your field.

Learn from Others' Mistakes

We all make mistakes. No matter how smart or skilled we are, they are inevitable. Of course, the most important thing is that we learn from them. One trick to help you avoid the suffering of having to make too many mistakes is that you can learn from the mistakes of others. Obviously, you can learn in this way by observing your surroundings and watching the mistakes other people make, then figuring out what you can do to avoid making them yourself. However, this opportunity to learn from others' mistakes requires you to be at the right place at the right time, to witness a mistake happening by chance. You will also need to have enough expertise to realize when mistakes have been made. This is clearly an inefficient process and unlikely to be the most fruitful path to learning.

Doesn't it make more sense to learn about the common mistakes people make in your field, or in whatever topic you are interested in, and then avoiding those? Do not misunderstand, as again, mistakes are likely to happen no matter what you do. And in fact, mistakes are not all bad. They present us with great learning opportunities – and can be highly beneficial in our development. Whenever I find myself getting upset about a mistake I made, I remind myself that this is a lesson learned, and that I do not have to worry about making that mistake again, because now I will be more careful and avoid making it in the future. Those personal lessons are the most valuable. However, through reading about other people's mistakes, you can absorb many lessons in the time it takes to read a book, without having to make them yourself. This is something many of us fail to fully realize. After learning from others' mistakes in this way, if you must still make your own, they can be new ones and present you with higher level learning opportunities.

These are a few book titles that focus on learning from others' mistakes: *Brilliant Blunders* by Mario Livio, *Bad Days in History* by Michael Farquhar, and *Mistakes I Made at Work* by Jessica Bacal.

Pursue Your Own Education

A common fallacy is that your education ends with high school or college, but in today's world, the day your education ends is the day you become obsolete. Someone else who continues to learn will end up being promoted over you and you may eventually even lose your job if you stop learning new things. And when you lose that job, you will not be competitive enough to find a new job easily. This is because the people who were making sure to learn something new will be more competitive applicants than you. It is practical to be a lifelong learner for the above reasons, but it is also a joy if you allow yourself to be guided by your own personal curiosity. It is better to be guided by a love of learning something new than a fear of losing your job. As a benefit, if you learn something new regularly, then you will always have options in your career and life.

When you pursue your own education, you will not need to enroll in a classroom, and you will not necessarily need to pursue a degree or find a specific teacher or tutor to learn something. You will learn the most valuable skill, which is being able to learn on your own. When you pursue your own education through books, you will learn to figure out what your strengths and weaknesses are, what you need to know more about, what your deep interests are, and what is a waste of time and energy and not useful for you to know. You will be forced to think deeply about exactly what it is you want to accomplish and what you need to learn to do so, instead of blindly reading books that are assigned to you by someone else, with a purpose that someone else has for you.

The education with the highest value is the one that you pursue on your own. As an adult, you do not need someone to tell you what to learn. You are fully capable of deciding what it is that you want to learn and understand. You can decide whether your biggest priority is your relationships, your finances, that you want to pursue a new type of job, or if you want to learn more deeply about philosophy, history, or the sciences simply to grow in your understanding. A key in pursuing your own education will be in realizing what you know and do not know. Then you can read more of what you do not know that interests you. But you should not jump ahead too quickly – allow yourself to make progress gradually. If you have jumped into a topic which is too difficult for you to process, you can instead pursue something that is lighter or more fundamental, where the ideas are explained more thoroughly. Establish your foundation of understanding first and build up gradually from there. With practice, you will learn to pursue the right amount of challenge to stimulate your mind without overwhelming it.

Stimulate Your Creativity and Imagination

Most of this book will pertain to nonfiction reading, but I am still a big believer in the value of reading fiction. Fiction will be especially useful for stimulating our creativity and imaginations – thinking styles which will only become more and more valuable in the modern age. One reason for this is employability, as people who are creative are capable of creating their own jobs during difficult times. Another reason is that the most challenging problems humans face will not be solved by straightforward logic. If they were, we would have already figured them out. Rather, the biggest problems we face will require a creative and imaginative mindset, which can be cultivated through reading stories.

When we read, especially fiction or narrative nonfiction, we develop our abilities to imagine other worlds and lives. As a writer creates a world or universe through words, you are provided with the task of making those words come to life in your mind. You will imagine a world that is different from every other reader because you have your own unique imaginative abilities. When we watch TV or movies, rather, we do not need to exercise our imaginations in this way because the visual effects are provided for us. With movies we are processing the stimuli, whereas with books we are co-creating a world or a universe with the author. The author has provided the baseline information, but we must create the stimuli and imagery in our minds. Ultimately, through reading stories and exercising your creativity, you will be able to imagine more and more possible scenarios in your everyday life. A key benefit is that you will be more likely to come up with solutions when others get stuck.

Another important aspect of fiction books is that they tend to have no real limits in terms of where you can go. You can see what the Wild West was like, time travel, visit aliens, defy the laws of physics, solve crimes, and so forth. There are no limits to what can be experienced through reading. And many of these scenarios are so wildly different from your day to day life that of course they will stimulate your creativity and imagination. For deeply imaginative stories, read *Alice's Adventures in Wonderland* by Lewis Carroll, *Gulliver's Travels* by Jonathan Swift, or *The Hitchhiker's Guide to the Galaxy* by Douglas Adams.

Build Your Empathy and Understanding

In our day to day life, it is easy to forget that we are all thinking beings, with our own personal quirks, likes, loves, sensitivities, desires, and fears. There are such deep complexities to each and every one of us, but when we see a stranger in public, all we see is a superficial figure, and we rarely perceive the full complexities of a person. Even for the people that we know all of our lives such as a parent, sibling, or close friend, we do not truly know all the levels of complexity that make them who they are. For instance, we cannot access their innermost thoughts, besides of course what they choose to share with us.

But through reading, we can gain a greater insight into the essence of a fictional character or even the soul of a real person. And if the story is well done, we see that this person is as complex as we are. You can perceive their thoughts, feelings, perceptions, and you can essentially see the world through their eyes. This forces you as the reader to realize that: *Perhaps everyone is as deeply complex as I am, and I should see people as more than the superficial levels that I am able to perceive. Maybe I should be more empathetic and understanding, because at the end of the day I do not fully know what problems or sufferings other people are going through. They may have greater troubles than me.*

Expand Your Communication Skills

In my youth, I always enjoyed having something new to read and learning regularly. Since around 15 years of age, I realized that my reading habit had a great influence on my vocabulary and on my ability to articulate exactly what I wanted to say. At that time, I did not talk very much as I was more of an introvert, so I certainly could not attribute my growing vocabulary and articulation to speaking more than anyone else. It was due to reading. Not only was I articulating my own thoughts better, but I found that more and more often, I was able to help clarify the thoughts of my friends and family, on the occasions when they struggled to convey exactly what they wished. I had gained the ability to intuit what people truly meant when they spoke, not just focusing on the actual words used. This is an important skill when reading books too. What is the hidden meaning beneath the words, that not even the words themselves can fully capture? Have you ever pondered that?

When it comes to communication skills, something of key importance is knowing how to say exactly what is on your mind. Reading more and building your vocabulary helps with this. In my later teens as I read higher level books, I tended to use a full range of words, rather than just the most common ones. As you read more, you will naturally come up with the perfect word in some instances, when someone else would stumble, knowing the idea, but not being aware of which word conveys that idea. The language we use every day tends to be rather basic, suffering from overuse of the same words and ideas day after day. Even if we know words which are more precise, we tend to use lower level words because they feel safe and convenient. The issue is that sometimes these words do not allow us to convey *exactly* what we mean.

Through books, we can be exposed to a much deeper vocabulary, as authors tend to have a much more expansive vocabulary than the average person, and they find it important to use more accurate and descriptive words even if these are not always commonly known. Aside from reading, another helpful tip is to surround yourself by readers and people who have a richer vocabulary.

As you read more, you will learn about the powerful differences between words. There are nuances of meaning that can be significant between different words that you will learn to recognize. Is he *apathetic* or *nonchalant? Steadfast* or *intransigent? Introverted* or *introspective?* Are you unsure of what some of these words mean? Look them up. The more words you are exposed to, the more you learn to see them as having their own special quality, and you see the world in a richer and more vibrant way. Words are not mostly synonyms that all mean the same thing. They actually convey slightly different meanings that can become important, and in some cases, you can even misunderstand something deeply if you are not alert to specific meanings.

To become a better communicator, learn the deeper meanings (e.g., first, second, and third definitions) of the words that you use and that you hear or read. When you find yourself disagreeing about what a word means with someone, look it up. Often, you will find that a word has several meanings, some of which may even conflict with one another. One such word is *abysmal*, which usually means *horrible*, but can also mean *profound*. One meaning implies something bad, and the other something neutral or good. A tip is that when you hear someone use a word and you think she used it incorrectly – do not correct her immediately, some people will use the second or third definition of the word which is lesser known, catching you off guard. Also, if you hear the same word used often, even in unrelated situations, look it up. People may be using the word incorrectly without being aware of this.

To be clear, expanding your vocabulary is not about showing off the words you know. No one will be impressed. This is about expanding your ability to think more precisely. It is difficult to think of something unless you know the specific words that relate to that thought. *Imagine:* How can you think of what "North" and "South" are if you do not already have a basic understanding of magnetism and the shape of the Earth? As you *build your vocabulary*, you will be able to *think more precisely*, which will help you to better *communicate your ideas* to others. After you have learned to communicate exactly what you wish to say, the next skill that will be important for you to learn is to communicate complex ideas in basic terms, so that everyone can understand.

The Reading Simulator

The act of reading is like entering a simulator, allowing you to experience the bad paths that lead to negative consequences, and the good paths that lead to positive outcomes. As a pilot will enter a simulator to practice flying, a human being will enter the simulator of reading books to practice living life. Through such simulated experiences we are able to discover a great amount about ourselves. Perhaps you find a role model in a character or person you are reading about – and decide you want to follow in his steps. Conversely, you may read about real-life villains or fictional ones and decide that you never want to be that way. Perhaps you see that someone puts himself in a very difficult situation and you realize that you would never put yourself in such a compromising position. The benefit with books is that you can read about all the different ways to live your life and see what the options are, instead of simply doing what you have always done, or rather than doing what you have always seen done around you. *Reading expands the boundaries of what we can think, be, see, and do.* Ultimately, through reading you can shut off the aspects of life that are unimportant or irrelevant to you and magnify the parts of life that have the potential to offer infinite paths of joy and opportunity for you. A major benefit of reading is that we can discover who we truly are, what we are in this world to do, and then we can set out to do it productively.

Reading Habits, Approaches, and Styles

An Introduction

In this section we will learn about the best reading habits, approaches, and styles that we should work on developing. Most of us learn to read at a very young age, but soon after this we do not continue to receive tips for how to become better readers. If we have classes on reading, often we are given material to read and then we are quizzed on what we read, but we are not given much guidance on how to develop better reading habits and skills in general. We are left to our own devices to figure this out, and for many of us, we may continue to have the same approach to reading for all of our lives. However, I think our reading abilities are important enough that we should spend some time to think them through and make sure that we are always making progress.

The Data – Trends in Reading

How much do most people actually read? The average American reads 12 books per year, which seems good, but in fact this number is influenced by a small percentage of people who read a lot. The median number of books read is just 4, which is closer to the number of books most people actually read. This means that half of people will read at least 4 books per year, and half of people will read less.

What do we mean when we say "read"? In 2018, 72% of U.S. adults read a book in any format, 65% read a print book, 25% read an eBook, and 20% listened to an audiobook. The general trend is that people have been reading paperback books and eBooks at about the same rate for many years, and more people have been listening to audiobooks as time goes on.

Here are some further trends to consider: women read more, younger people read more, people with more formal education read more, and people who earn more money also read more. These are trends and not necessarily rules. Certainly, there are people from all walks of life who are readers.

The above data is according to www.pewresearch.org

Read More and Do Not Make Excuses

This is the ultimate reading habit. If you do not make it a priority to read on a regular basis, it is too easy for everything else to take precedence over reading. We make time for TV, social media, other forms of entertainment, yet we often fail to read, and we regress in our lives when this happens. When we are not reading, we neglect to learn new things, to invest in our personal growth, and to pursue a path toward our best selves. The habit of regular reading can help us with such matters of importance, but somehow, we put it on the backburner, as if it were just another trivial activity in our lives. Instead, we must enlighten ourselves as to the true importance of reading and make time for it. Most people understand the idea that they should invest money to grow their bank accounts, but we should also invest in ourselves through books to aid in our personal growth. If you do not choose to invest in yourself, who will?

Let's discuss a few ways to think about reading so that we can always make sure we are on the right path to including reading in our lives.

Using reason helps to guide me to make sure that I read regularly. I often think that watching a sitcom certainly will not be helping me in 5 or 10 years. That is time wasted compared to the insights I could be gaining through reading a book. Or I will think that this is a very competitive world. If I am *not* reading, I am falling behind the competition. Whereas if I am reading, I am always gaining an edge and putting myself in a better position to make progress and succeed in my goals. I will also think that there is limited time in my life – I want to learn as much as I can and in order to accomplish this, I must make time for regular reading.

Reasoning out why I should be doing something helps me, but it does not work for everyone. Many people need emotional triggers to get them to change their habits. In that case, consider the happiness or improved way of life you could achieve through reading. Or consider the major problems in your life that could vanish if you became a student of life and found solutions. Our lives will often flow in cycles, where we perpetually create the same problems for ourselves, over and over – wouldn't you rather read and find a way to beat your personal problematic cycles? If it helps, consider what could go wrong in your life as a result of *not* spending some time reading. *What catastrophic mistake might you be on the verge of making right now?* Remember that for any problem you have, someone has likely dealt with it and written a book on how to resolve it.

The benefits of reading are simply too great to ignore. If you struggle to make time to read, then listen to an audiobook on your commute to work or while you eat your lunch. If you do not have the money to spend on books, go to a library or swap books with friends. You can even use a site like Paperbackswap.com to trade books with people online. Free digital files of some books are also available online at sites such as Gutenberg.org.

As another example, perhaps you are easily distracted by noise when reading, and this prevents you from making progress. Then use noise-cancelling headphones and play light music, white noise, or the sounds of nature. Otherwise, simply go to a quiet place such as the library to do your reading. Distractions are a part of everyday life, so if this is something that is disrupting your ability to stick to your reading habit, then it will be well worth it to find a way to resolve the problem. As annoying as distractions can be, I have found that focusing on reading in spite of environmental sounds and noises has helped me to build my ability to focus.

Schedule Reading into Your Calendar

We already established that reading is a highly beneficial use of your time, which means that it will be worth it to schedule blocks of time into your calendar where you will sit and read or otherwise reflect on your readings and take notes on them. I schedule reading for one hour per day, usually at night from 9-10. Google Calendar (a free application) is convenient for this since I can easily setup repeating events, but you may use any calendar. Of course, schedule your reading for the time that works best for you. You can also split up your reading, doing part of it in the morning, and part in the evening if you prefer. If you are starting to get into the habit of reading, you may start with scheduling 15 minutes per day, to make sure you set an achievable goal.

I learned the importance of scheduling what you want to accomplish by reading *15 Secrets Successful People Know About Time Management* by Kevin Kruse. **The science says that scheduling what you want to do in a planner or calendar is more productive than having to-do lists.** Think about it: when you schedule something, it seems more important, as normally we schedule appointments and meetings that that we must attend. Thus, when we schedule our plans on a calendar, we feel more committed to working on those tasks. This insight has been very helpful not only for my reading goals, but also for helping me to be more productive in my personal and work goals.

How Many Books Should You Read?

This is a typical question, yet the answer will be different for everyone. As a starting point, you may begin with the goal of reading one book per month. Most of us can reach this pace if we put some effort into building a reading routine. After you have succeeded with this, try reading two per month. Reading one or two books per month is a great accomplishment, but if you have already achieved this, you can strive for reading three or four books per month. My goal is to read about three books per month, but you are welcome to pursue a goal that works for you. In the end, you should feel free to go on your own reading journey, in your own way.

The important thing is to make a goal and stick with it, progressing slowly if you like, as this is often more productive than making sudden changes that you are unable to keep up with. To help you keep pace with reading the number of books you wish to read, you may find it useful to limit the book sizes you will read to anywhere from 250 to 500 pages, depending on your preference. In time as you get into the rhythm of reading more books, you can stop limiting the page amounts. For example, many years ago, I used to limit myself to books that were no longer than 500 pages. This was because I was eager to read as many books as I could at the time. I no longer focus on the number of pages or the number of books, as now I put more emphasis on what I am learning and gaining from what I read. Nonetheless, if a book is over 500 pages, I will examine it more closely to try to ensure that it will be a worthwhile read, since it will use up much more of my time.

What if You Struggle to Make the Time to Read?

If you struggle to find time to read, use the system presented in *The Miracle Morning* by Hal Elrod, where reading is an activity so important that you spend some time on it every morning when you wake up. Instead of reaching for your phone and flipping through social media or checking emails, you can invest in yourself first. Even if it is 10-15 minutes of reading time, this is still beneficial. Perhaps you can also schedule some time later in the day to read. But in case you never get back to it, you can rest assured that you made progress on your reading goals first thing in the morning.

In *The Miracle Morning*, a key insight I learned was that **it is important for us to prioritize our wellbeing much higher than most of us do. Spending some time in the mornings on important self-developmental goals can go a long way toward improving our lives.** If we wake up and start the day dreading having to go to work, checking emails that we do not really want to read, and flipping through social media in a zombie state, then we are starting the day in the wrong frame of mind. Also, this is clearly not helping our general wellbeing. Instead, we should start each day doing something beneficial for ourselves, such as reading something of value, exercising, meditating, or journaling. This may mean getting up a half hour early every day and cutting off your time to watch a TV show at night, but ultimately taking deeper care of ourselves will help to improve every facet of our lives.

What if your struggle is not finding the time, but it has more to do with your difficulties in staying motivated and focused enough to continue reading? In such cases, understand that the more you read, the more background information you will gain to make sense of new books that you read. I have read many, many books on psychology, self-development, writing, and business, so if I choose to read a book in any of these topics, I am able to acquire any new knowledge from the pages quite efficiently. I will quickly see that I am highly familiar with a certain chapter, so then I can refresh myself on certain topics for that chapter instead of reading everything in painstaking detail. Also, I can focus on reading more interesting and advanced books, rather than becoming bored with the dry fundamentals of a topic. Although reading may be a struggle early on, it will get easier as you read more and find more patterns, learn more, understand more, and acquire more insights to help you learn more efficiently.

If you struggle to read regularly and stick with it, find an accountability partner – preferably one who also wants to improve her reading habits and abilities. You do not even need to read the same book. You can talk weekly about what you are reading, what you are getting out of it, and the type of progress you are making with your reading goals. Finding a partner to help support you is one of the best steps you can take in life with any area that is important to you, especially when you are truly struggling to make progress. This may be the push you need to make a positive change in your life.

Surround Yourself with Different Books for Different Purposes

You may have comic books for reading something that is entertaining for both yourself and your children. You may also read thrillers with your spouse to discuss the stories together. In addition, perhaps you are reading some technical materials on different types of plants for your work or to help with your personal garden. And you may be reading Albert Einstein's biography (e.g., *Einstein: His Life and Universe* by Walter Isaacson) to learn about his life and what helped him make his great discoveries. Of course, different people have different limits as to how many books they will read side by side. You may prefer to only read one book at a time and someone else may read several at a time, but the key point here is to always have something that you are in the mood to read. Perhaps you usually read one book at 9PM, but on this night you are not in the mood for that book. You always want to have something to read that you are excited about, or you will procrastinate and find something else to do. Also, waiting can be a big part of modern life. But sometimes when you are waiting (e.g., on your commute or at the doctor's office), you are not in the mood to read something too difficult or dense. For those situations, you should have something lighter that you can read through easily and save the more difficult readings for when you can truly focus.

It is also a good idea to read in different formats. I prefer to read some books in paper, some in eBook form, and some as audiobooks. For instance, I recently began reading *In Search of Lost Time* by Marcel Proust, and I had a difficult time focusing through the elaborate and long-winded prose, so I decided that this would be better to read in audio format, and I have found it to be a much more enjoyable experience this way. My preferred format is to read in paper, but eBooks are also very convenient and so often I read them. I have also found it helpful to have an audiobook or two saved that I can listen to when I want to savor the reading experience. Having access to a variety of book formats helps to create an environment where I am always surrounded by books and I have no real excuse to not read. Surround yourself with a wide range of books for different purposes, and you will never have an excuse to avoid reading. This will help you to cultivate a regular reading habit.

Build Your Anti-library

Nassim Nicholas Taleb writes in *The Black Swan*, "A private library is not an ego-boosting appendage but a research tool. Read books are far less valuable than unread ones. The library should contain as much of what you do not know as your financial means, mortgage rates and the currently tight real-estate market allows you to put there. You will accumulate more knowledge and more books as you grow older, and the growing number of unread books on the shelves will look at you menacingly. Indeed, the more you know, the larger the rows of unread books. Let us call this collection of unread books an anti-library."

It is easy to feel bad for acquiring piles of books that you may not have read fully or read at all, but I would encourage you to not feel too bad. As noted above, the books you have not read are the ones with the greatest potential value for you. They contain knowledge and wisdom that you do not yet know, and thus are portals to your greater understanding. If you are able, it is an excellent idea to surround yourself with books that have the potential to be highly useful to you. If your dream is to become an artist, then you can surround yourself with books about art history, analysis of artworks, and instructions on art technique. Or if you love literature, you may surround yourself with some of the most celebrated classics of all time. You can acquire such books gradually and pick and choose to read them at the time that you wish. The most important books are the ones that we end up reading and applying in our lives – and those are likely to be the ones that we surround ourselves with.

Keep in mind that there can also be value in having a digital library that you can take with you easily, wherever you go. You can gain subscribe to services such as Scribd or Kindle Unlimited if you would like access to vast amounts of digital books. An alternative is to check with your local or national libraries – sometimes you can have access to a large digital catalog online. If you prefer paper books, the only practical way to surround yourself with these is to buy them. To save money, you may consider going to used book shops. It may even be best to do both if you are able – have a digital library as well as a physical one so that you always have access to quality reading material, whether you are at home or traveling.

Keep Track of Your Books

One of the best ways to improve your behavior in any area of your life is to keep track of what you are doing. For example, if you keep track of your books, and you see that you have not read anything in half a year, it is quite easy to see that you should focus on making some improvements in your reading habits.

Books you have read

Keeping track of the books you have read will help you to ensure that you are making progress with your goals. Perhaps you will find that 9 out of 10 books you read are actually comics or in the romance genre, and you would like to read books that have more substance. Or perhaps you feel that you are well-read in history, but you find that you actually abandon most of the history books that you begin, making your knowledge of the topic questionable. By keeping track of what you read, you will discover such flaws in your tendencies.

Books you want to read

Make sure you have books on this list that you are truly excited about, that you cannot wait to begin reading. There should be so many great books on your list that you do not even know where to start. There is no need to worry if you do not have your list developed right now, because surely you will get there in time. When you are starting, it is important that you remember to write down any books that catch your interest, as you do not want to forget about them. Do not be too critical about which books you allow on your list to read. If there is something of value or of interest in the book, add it. Later when you are deciding what to read, you can scrutinize the books more carefully. If you decide that a book is ultimately not worthwhile, you can always remove it from your list. Keep in mind that you may have separate lists if this helps your organization, such as "Maybe to-reads" and "Definite to-reads."

The best and most insightful books you have read

It is important to keep a list of your best books because often, these books still have information and insights that you will want to review. Some books are so useful and beneficial that it is difficult to fully appreciate, understand, and apply them after reading them once. You will want to reread them and review any notes you have taken to make sure that you internalize the message of the book. Your best books will also likely be the ones that you find most important to recommend to others, to help improve their lives.

You should update this list of books regularly, as a book that you find insightful now may not be very insightful to you in 10 years, when you have hopefully had the opportunity to reach a much deeper level of understanding.

Goodreads

I have been recording the books I read, the books I want to read, and the most insightful books I have read on Goodreads for about a decade, and I have been quite happy with the application. Of course, you may use another app, or you could even keep track of these on your own if you wish. There are many additional benefits to Goodreads such as being able to build or join communities of readers, and best of all it is free. If you need some help using the site or app, go to YouTube and search "How to use Goodreads" or "Goodreads tutorial."

Read Widely

Many readers lean toward reading mostly fiction, or mostly nonfiction, but we sometimes fail to realize that there are great benefits to both types of reading. Through fiction you can improve your imagination and see more of the potential for either heroism or wrongdoing in humanity. These are the stories that capture the universal human condition and help to reveal what it truly means to be a human being. With nonfiction, you are able to learn more about any specific topic that may be of interest to you. You will usually study a topic directly in the form of concepts, rules, and facts, whereas with fiction, often the theme that the book is meant to make you think about is only revealed to you after major plot events transpire. With nonfiction, you may feel that you are learning as if a student being taught by a teacher, and with fiction you may feel that you are learning as if you have been given the chance to simulate someone else's life and learn valuable life lessons in this way. Through reading nonfiction, you are provided with a guide, or documentation of something that happened and the lessons that may be learned from it. With fiction, things rarely go according to plan and you learn lessons from the problems that arise and how they are dealt with. I prefer to read mostly nonfiction, but I have learned that it is a mistake to assume that we cannot learn greatly through reading fiction as well.

Consider that the terms "fiction" and "nonfiction" can actually be ironic, as I have found that often the most profound truths are available through fiction, and the most profound distortions of truth are found in nonfiction. Understand that just because a book is in the nonfiction section does not make it true, and just because it is in the fiction section does not make it false. Of course, in fiction the stories may be made up, but the lessons, concepts, and depictions of humanity and society can be all too real. And perhaps a nonfiction book is made up of all true stories, but the people in the book could be falsely characterized, only giving you a narrow and misleading perspective of what happened. Or the author may exaggerate certain pieces of information, making you assume that the book is more useful and applicable than it is. My point is that fiction and nonfiction are vague terms that do not fully capture the different types of readings that are available to us. Even if you prefer to read mostly nonfiction, make sure to read some fiction, and vice versa.

Whether you read fiction or nonfiction or both, it is also a good idea to read in a wide variety of book topics. For example, there is science, history, self-development, philosophy, current affairs, science fiction, literary fiction, poetry, historical fiction, and so forth. The more widely you read, the more you will see concepts that interrelate and can be applied to different areas. Someone who reads widely will ultimately be a better conversationalist, more creative, and better able to understand a wide variety of topics. Life is more interesting when you can make sense of many different aspects of it, and you are not limited to understanding only one or two domains.

When reading nonfiction, hunt for insights, whereas with fiction you must be patient and trust that the story will take you somewhere fulfilling and be open to where the journey takes you. Understand that both types of reading require different approaches, or you may be left disappointed.

Read Different Books Differently, Depending on Your Purpose

Shallow reading

This is an exploratory form of reading that you employ when you want to learn the basic idea of a book. You may skim the table of contents, flip through the book and pay more attention to headings, bullet points, summary sections, key terms, or anything else that captures your attention. You will ask yourself questions such as: *Is this book truly worth investing my time and energy into? Does this book meet my needs right now? Does it have interesting ideas I may want to come back to later?*

Surgical reading

This is a reading style you will apply when you have a very specific purpose that you want to achieve. For example, maybe you want to lose five pounds of fat in a week, while not losing muscle. Also, you only have two hours of reading time because you are too busy with other tasks for the coming week. This is a specific goal with a time constraint where you may want to consult a few different books, keeping in mind your particular goal and ignoring the rest of the information which does not apply. I call this surgical reading because you will focus on your goal with surgical precision. As the surgeon aims to effect only one part of the body and nothing else during an operation, you will aim to learn *only* what is necessary for your specific goal.

Practical reading

This is the type of reading you will use for many books that focus on tips for how to do something. For example, you are likely employing *practical reading* now. With practical reading, you will have a general goal such as to make friends, to get a promotion at work, or to improve your abilities in something. With this goal in mind, you will collect the tips that you feel are most important, and then apply them in your life. Then you will gauge if the tips are working effectively for you. If they are not, you may reread the book to see if you misunderstood something or misapplied the tips, or you may pursue other books or information instead.

Comprehension reading

Typically, you will apply this reading style with books that are densely packed with information, or which cover a challenging topic. For such books, do not be in a rush to understand everything all at once – this may take time to accomplish. With comprehension reading, your goal above all else is to make sure you have understood the author's message. *When he describes or defines a key term, do you understand? When he describes relationships between people or systems or ideas, is this clear?* You want to make sure you follow the logic, arguments, and the way that he links ideas together. When you miss something, you will want to go back and make sure that you followed the main ideas before continuing forward.

Deep reading

To read deeply, do not read just one book on a topic and then feel that you have mastered it. If a topic is truly important to you, read many books about it to gain different perspectives. Keep in mind that sometimes one author has one perspective, and other authors may have contrary perspectives, and all of these authors may be experts in their fields yet still conflict in their opinions. When you have read many books in a topic, you are no longer taking information at face value – you are instead comparing whether a new piece of knowledge fits well into the prior mental map (e.g., your perception of how ideas interrelate) you had developed for a given field.

Another way to read deeply is instead of reading more, to spend more time reading a single important book and reflecting on what it means. You may read one book two or more times, or spend time carefully thinking about a book, taking notes, applying the contents and discussing it with colleagues, rather than automatically jumping from one book to the next. Reading more is not always the goal, so do not feel that you are not making progress because someone else has read more books. If you learned more and acquired a greater level of understanding from books that were important to you and that was your goal, then you are well on your road to progress in your reading journey.

Generally, this style of reading will require much more attention, deliberation, and effort on your part. However, for a truly insightful book, you will likely want to employ this form of reading, to make sure that you benefit the most that you possibly can.

This is the focus of *The Insightful Reader* – to pursue the books with the most insights, and then to read them deeply so that we can absorb and understand those insights. If we do this, hopefully we will then become insightful readers.

Immersive reading

When you find a book that you adore, or a really good page-turner, you will likely employ *immersive reading*. Here, you will become so absorbed with what you are reading that you will be transported into another world. Often, this happens with fiction, but it can also occur with narrative nonfiction or perhaps other books. When this happens to you, allow the story to take you on a journey without resisting what is happening. For these special types of books do not worry if you are reading optimally. If your mind is fully engaged and you are completely absorbed in the story, it is quite likely that you are understanding or experiencing the book on a higher level, and there is no need to interrupt your flow. When you have finished the book, reflect on what it all means and employ some of the techniques discussed in this book. Keep in mind that if you feel that you have missed something important after practicing immersive reading, you can always go back and reread the book more deeply.

Aim to Gather Insights, Not Just Collect Meaningless Facts

A big mistake people make when they read is that they see a book as just a way to acquire facts. I would argue that we need to change this way of thinking. Do not look to memorize facts, instead read for understanding and especially, *read to gain insights*. **If there is one key insight you take away from this book, it is that you should *read for insights, not just facts.*** The facts can change quickly in the modern era, but insights tend to endure and stand the test of time. If you think that the prior statement sounds silly, remember that a fact is only a fact until proven otherwise. In the modern age, often the facts that we learn must be unlearned, as new and more accurate facts are discovered by researchers and practitioners. Therefore, patterns of facts that support an insight will be more important to us, rather than the individual facts themselves.

Let's clarify what I mean by "insights," as this is very important. **Insights present you with a shift in the way you think about an idea or topic. They provide you with a realization that you should change the way you think about something and reconsider the actions that you take.** Keep in mind that an insight for you is not necessarily an insight for someone else, or vice versa. Ultimately, an insight is personally meaningful to you.

Facts do matter, of course, but do not see the contents of a book as just chains of facts that you need to remember. Do not read as if you are going to be given a test in school. Instead, look at sets of facts that support something truly important, and pay attention to those. For instance, if you have an insight – such as that some animals deserve the same rights as humans – then you may need to justify this with facts or a line of reasoning to yourself or to someone else.

Here is an example of facts you may use to support this insight: We aim to give all humans basic rights regardless of their intellect and regardless of any kind of disability they may have. There are some animals of some species that will be of a higher intellect or of a higher ability than some humans (e.g., some disabled individuals), thus we should either treat some humans as lesser than humans, which seems ridiculous, or we should treat some animals as having the same rights as humans. This leads us to the insight that some animals deserve the same rights as humans.

I do not claim that the above line of reasoning is correct or that there are no possible counterarguments. Rather, this is meant as an example of an insight someone may have, and the possible supporting facts or line of reasoning that would go along with the insight. You do not need to remember *all* the facts that support your insights, but do make sure to remember the most important ones.

The way you know that a book is truly worthwhile is if it provides you with an insight. If there is an insight in a book that you had not had before, then the book will be valuable to you. Do not assume that insights will come from *only* classical works or highly dense and difficult reads. They could come from a graphic novel, a cookbook, or a light and humorous science fiction book. Insights can even come from general experiences that you have in life, from a mentor, or from learning something new. But in my experience, the most insights and the greatest insights will come from reading quality books. When you are a serious reader, you will make it your job to hunt for them and aim to read more quality books.

Challenge Your Point of View

Do not simply read books that already support what you think about the world. If you are convinced that one political party is better, read a book from the perspective of the other party. If you have always assumed that science had all the answers and was the ultimate truth, read a book that expresses the importance of mysticism, religions, or spiritualism. If you believe that lower level workers are the most important part of an organization, then read a book that shows the perspective of CEOs and other leaders in big corporations.

I am not asking you to believe everything you read, but it is a great intellectual exercise to hold conflicting thoughts in mind where at first you think *I know this to be false, because it contradicts my long-held beliefs* to then thinking *maybe parts of this are true and I need to learn more*, and if not, perhaps you can get to a point where you think *this is an interesting perspective although it is not for me, but at least now I know more about how some people think and feel about the topic.*

As humans, we need to focus on understanding other people more – even if they may have completely different perspectives from us. At some point, we need to learn that *we do not have the one right way of viewing the world* – there are many other ways to see things. And we do not always need to focus on all the differences that we have, and to villainize each other – perhaps we can try to see what common frame of reference or understanding we can build upon instead. If you are convinced that you know everything and that anyone who thinks differently is wrong, it will be very difficult for you to learn something new. We must cultivate more open minds, so we can prepare to gain the most insights on our reading journey.

To Finish a Book or Not?

This is not always as straightforward of a choice as it may seem. Some people finish every book they begin, and others abandon more books than they finish. I tend to finish most books that I start, but if I feel that the value is very low and I come to doubt that there are any insights for me to acquire, I will ultimately abandon a book. Another reason I will not finish a book is if I feel that there are much higher quality books for me to invest my time into, or if a pressing problem arises that I want to read about more thoroughly.

I would caution you against abandoning a book simply because it is difficult to understand. A highly skilled reader will need to finish some books that are difficult to read, and eventually those difficult-to-read books will become easier and easier to make sense of with experience. Of course, I judge such difficult books by whether useful insights can be acquired from them. Be aware that often, older classical books can be more difficult to understand, but they are also more likely to provide us with profound insights. The language used may be more difficult or more complicated than we are used to, but it can still provide you with great benefits if you are willing to push through until you fully grasp the author's key points.

Keep in mind that sometimes it is simply not the right time for you to read a book. I have found certain books too much of a burden, put them aside, then come back to them a few years later only to find that I could not believe I was not captivated by the book on my first attempt. In one case it was *1984* by George Orwell. It may be fully understandable that I was not deeply interested in the book the first time I read it, as I was only 14 years old. The book started so slowly for me that I wondered how anyone could ever get through it or how it could even be considered a classic, and I gave up on it. Nonetheless, I was assigned to read it a few years later for a class and it made a huge impression on me. Now, it remains one of my favorite books. Another book was highly recommended to me by my cousin, *Guns, Germs, and Steel* by Jared Diamond. The first time I read it, I thought the topics were too dry and the writing simply did not hold my interest. I was forcing myself to get through the pages, and I ended up abandoning it without making much progress or learning much. When I came back to the book years later, it was one of the most impressive books I had ever read, providing me with insight after insight. I could hardly believe that this was the same book I had tried to read a few years earlier. The point here is that even if you set a book aside, always keep an open mind to it and realize that it may be worth coming back to later.

If you decide that a book is not worth fully reading, but you want to try to get some value from it, perhaps an insight you had overlooked or some key piece of information as to why this book matters, consider reading the introduction to gain a context of what the book is about, and then the conclusion (for nonfiction only). Often, if there are insights in the book, they will at least be mentioned within the conclusion – but to fully understand and make use of those insights, you will likely need to read more of the book. Also, if there are summary points or concluding thoughts at the end of the chapters, you may read some of those. If after doing this, you struggle to understand how the book could be considered good by many people, it may help to read some reader reviews as well. Often, they will reveal some of the personal insights that they gained.

If some of the above suggestions pique your interest and you want to learn more, then feel free to read the rest of the book. If you have a general interest in it but you do not feel it will provide much value, you may just read the first and last page of every section to again get an overview, without needing to read all of the intermediate parts. Depending on how the book is structured, you may choose instead to read the first and last paragraph of each section. Remember, you are allowed to skip parts that are of little relevance or interest to you – you can read for efficiency. Throughout this process if the book piques your interest, you may decide that it is worth reading the book from front to back, or at least to read certain chapters more thoroughly. Another possibility is that you may have gained some value from this process but decide that the book is not worth reading more deeply, and that is fine too. You can move on to another one in that case.

Train Yourself to Sit Down and Read Mindfully

In the modern age we are perpetually busy, entertained, or distracted in some way. We are always doing something or plugged into something, and this means our minds get in the habit of always seeking a certain level of stimulation. This stimulation level is not easy to achieve through reading – and if you are beginning on your journey as a serious reader, then you may feel that reading can feel quite dull or boring at times. However, as you focus on becoming a better reader, your mind will become more and more stimulated through the act of reading. In time as you progress, your stimulation level through reading will exceed the stimulation you would have obtained through TV or other entertainment, which means you will come to prefer reading over such activities. You will likely find that the more you practice reading deeply and skillfully, the more enjoyable and useful the activity becomes. Reading provides you with a sort of mental gym – you cannot expect your path toward mental fitness to be easy in the beginning, you must push through to get to the other side.

As you become a more experienced reader, your mind will be going in many interesting directions as you read. You will be asking questions, thinking about how you can apply what you read, wondering more deeply what the author truly means by a phrase, considering if the book is too basic for you, and hunting for insights rather than passively absorbing individual facts. Your mind will learn to be more highly activated, more fully awake through your reading instead of teetering on the verge of falling asleep and boredom. This is the level of reading you should strive for.

As you read, if you find yourself becoming sleepy, sit up straight and practice waking up your mind, to think more actively as you read. You cannot read with the same mindset that you use when you passively take in a television program. The television is always producing the next piece of content for you – and often, lower level shows are making sure that everything is easy to digest and understand, to avoid making you have to think. With reading, you must be physically and mentally engaged, and often the material is not fully digested for you, as the author expects you to put in some work so that you can build your understanding.

If you find it difficult to sit quietly and concentrate on your reading, practice reading mindfully for 5 minutes per day, then build up to 10, 15, 20, 30 minutes, and so forth. To do this, clear away all distractions and keep your mind on the task of reading and understanding. If your mind drifts, return it to the act of reading. Train your mind to focus in this way, and you will build up your capacity to pay attention to something longer and longer. This will benefit you outside of reading as well, as your ability to focus will expand.

Choosing What to Read

An Introduction

As a child I sometimes felt anxious when I went to the library, as I often had a very difficult time choosing what to read. Sometimes the librarians would try to help, but even with assistance, choosing between different books was not easy for me. Eventually, I found that some of my favorite books were the Choose Your Own Adventure series by R. A. Montgomery, Edward Packard and other authors, and the Goosebumps series by R. L. Stine. Generally, these were fast and fun reads. I read many books in these series, and I also read some other books that were written in a similar style. As the years passed, I moved on to classical fiction for children, but those fun books in my earlier years gave me the basic skills and joy for reading that kept me making progress toward more challenging and stimulating books. Finding a series you enjoy is an obvious way to help you choose what to read, but in this section we will cover more elaborate tips you can employ to help you decide what to read next.

Know Your Goal

Questions that can help to fine tune your reading goal

- Is the difficulty of the material worth the potential understanding and insights I can gain from it?
- Does this challenge me to learn something new?
- Will I use what I learn here in some way?
- Will this help me to improve my life or someone else's life?
- Can this information give me a new outlook on the world?
- Will this help me be more empathetic or understanding of different types of people?
- Is this book written for beginners, intermediates, or experts?

These are the types of questions I tend to ask when I am choosing a book to read – you are welcome to formulate your own questions as well.

It is generally useful to have a goal for what you want to accomplish with a book. If there is no goal, your mind may fall into an inactive state, flipping through the pages passively, not knowing what you are looking for. The mind always needs to have something to seek and pay attention to, or it can become dull and even confused. When you have a purpose, you should keep it in mind from the moment you begin to read. As an example, if you are reading a book on how to cook, your goal may be to learn five new recipes so that you can learn to cook by heart without too much difficulty, to prepare your own dinners for the week. This would mean that you could focus more on learning just the recipes that appeal to you, that are perhaps not too complicated, and that you feel you could learn quickly. When you learn those five recipes, you may write them down to help commit them to memory, and then practice cooking them to see if you like how they turn out. If some of them turn out poorly, you can go back to your book to search for a better recipe. The point here is that when you have something specific you want to accomplish, you will be much more efficient if you keep your focus. Someone who thinks, *I want to learn to cook*, and reads a full book on cooking and sets it aside, may easily forget the whole thing and never apply it. You will want to avoid this.

Perhaps you are more like me and you do not tend to have specific goals with everything you read – your goals are more like *to learn something new* or *to challenge yourself*. My goal when I read tends to be to gain a new insight that will change the way I see something, or to have an insight that I can use for my own benefit or for the benefit of others. For instance, the book *Mastery* by Robert Greene was a life-changing book that I read when I was 27 years old, and the most important insight I gained was that **pursuing a type of work that is meaningful to you and that you are driven to pursue is the best path you can take and will ultimately be the most fulfilling.** Reading this book made me realize that I had been too focused on wanting to earn income fast, and that instead if I were to focus on doing something that I found to be truly meaningful, this would ultimately provide me with the most happiness, personal growth, and likely even wealth – in the long-term. This may seem like a basic idea if you have already realized this, but to someone who is unsure of what path to pursue, this insight at the right moment can change a life.

Ask yourself on a deeper level what your life goals are. *Is your goal to fall in love? Is it to get fit and develop an exercise routine that you can stick to? Or is your goal to get your whole life organized – all of your digital and physical files, and everything you own?* Regardless of your goal, ask if this book will get you closer to accomplishing that. If not, keep searching until you find the right book that will help you to meet your goals.

In What Area of Life am I Bankrupt?

Here is the easiest way to figure out what to read next.

Ask yourself: **In what area of life am I bankrupt?**

Am I literally bankrupt, with no money to spend? Am I making poor ethical choices, always getting caught in lies and feeling guilty for my actions? Am I struggling to raise my kids properly? Do I find it difficult to make personal connections with anyone? Am I falling behind at work because I lack understanding in certain technical areas? Is my poor time management causing problems in many areas of my life? What aspect of your life is going so badly that you truly need help *now* to fix it? That is the topic that you should read about next. To do this right will take some self-reflection, but if you think deeply enough, you will likely find a major flaw in how you have been doing things, and that there is room for improvement in some area of your life.

Is This Worth Reading a Full Book on?

Before you decide to read a book, ask if you truly need a book's worth of information. For example, do you need to read 200+ pages about a topic to solve your problem? Perhaps you have one very specific issue, and you do not need to know the context, or you do not have the time to get into all of the details. In such a case, searching for an article, a video, a colleague, or some other source of information would be more beneficial.

Be aware that some books only contain about an article's worth of information in them, and the rest is padded out with fluff. Fluff is filler that does not provide you with much value. To me, fluff is a lack of insight. Since I am on the search for insight, I am also looking for fluff so that I can avoid it. If a book is mostly filler, I will usually choose not to read it, and keep looking for something that may provide me with more insights. There is a saying that one person's trash is another's treasure – likewise, one person's fluff is another's insight and vice versa. Only you can decide which is which.

Some books follow the pattern of providing a rule or principle, then give example after example in support of the principle. This can be helpful if those specific examples add extra value for you, but in other cases you may understand the point right away and not need to read through many examples. Perhaps reading a shorter article on the topic will make more sense in such cases. If you wish to find interesting articles to read, *Feedly* is a useful free site to manage your article subscriptions. I read articles and books regularly, as they can both be helpful for different purposes. Often, if you read an article that you are interested in, this can pique your interest and you may then wish to read a full book on the topic. Sometimes, the author of the article has also written books that you can consider reading.

On occasion, it may be worthwhile to read a fluffy book, but I recommend moving beyond this level as soon as you are ready, rather than staying stuck there. Consider these books to be written at a beginner level, and likely to have only one insight. Rather, if you read more dense and difficult materials, you are likely to obtain more insights and they are likely to be of higher value to you. But of course, such books will be more challenging as well.

What Types of Books Do You Prefer?

Perhaps you prefer writing that is concise and to the point, but you have found a book that rambles and overelaborates points that seem quite obvious to you. Rather than struggle through such books that you don't connect with, it could make more sense to pursue the books that are written in a way that appeals to you. To get a sense of the writing style, you can randomly open up the book and look at the size of sentences, the type of emotion or personality behind the writing, and whether the message is clear or needlessly complicated.

Also, ask yourself: Do you like it when books go into theoretical and abstract ideas, or do you prefer that everything stay in the practical and applied realm? Are you looking for simpler reads that anyone can understand, or more technical and academic reads that get into the fine details and nuances of specific issues? Do you prefer popular and widely read books so that you can join discussions with friends and neighbors, or do you prefer to acquire unique knowledge that may not be known to most people? Would you like more stories, or more principles? More logic, or more emotion?

To find the best books for you, you have to be aware of your own preferences.

What is the Shelf Life of the Information in the Book?

For extremely hot, trendy, or technologically focused areas, the information may quickly become outdated, and due to the time it takes to write and publish a book, it may be out of date by the time the book is published. For example, a book about a specific computer program may fail to consider a new update to the software. Such books are still useful if they involve your work or something that you need to know. But for fields where the information is frequently changing, it can be more useful to find information online that may be updated more often, as opposed to a book which will probably not be updated often, if at all.

Generally, as you pick up a book or read its description or table of contents, ask if this information will still be relevant to you or to the world in five years. The world is rapidly changing, but if you spend a lot of time reading materials that will be irrelevant in five years, you may be wasting too much of your time instead of making true progress in your life.

The history of information has shown us that if we wait long enough, the things that we thought we knew eventually turn out to be false in some way. Of course, science helps us make progress in that we gradually discover rules, facts, and patterns that show us something closer to the truth. At this point, much of our information and knowledge likely has truth in it, but we may find in the years or decades to come that we made improper assumptions which made much of our information irrelevant, or we may find that our understanding was limited in scope and failed to take into account an important context or system. Perhaps our environment is changing fast enough that the information which used to apply will no longer be relevant within a new, rapidly changing context. Ask yourself: *Is the context changing fast enough that the book I am reading will be obsolete quite soon?*

What Books Have Helped the People That You Look up to?

Whoever you respect or look up to, ask them what they have read that made a big impression on them. For example, is there a leader who you admire? You may look up to certain people who are also public figures, and perhaps they have websites where they discuss important books they have read. Simply put this in your search engine: "[Name] favorite books," or you can try "[Name] book recommendations."

This is a major shortcut for finding the books that will be truly important and worthwhile for you. If a book made a big impression on someone that you respect and admire, there is a good chance that this book will make a big impact on you and be filled with useful insights.

The following are examples of books that made an impact on some well-known people:

Chimamanda Adichie: *Arrow of God* by Chinua Achebe
Maya Angelou: *Look Homeward, Angel* by Thomas Wolfe
Jeff Bezos: *Lean Thinking* by James Womack
Jorge Luis Borges: *Amerika* by Franz Kafka
Warren Buffet: *Business Adventures* by John Brooks
Paulo Coelho: *The Stranger* by Albert Camus

Matt Damon: *A People's History of the United States* by Howard Zinn
Bob Dylan: *The Life and Times of Sonny Barger and the Hell's Angels Motorcycle Club* by Sonny Barger
Albert Einstein: *A Treatise of Human Nature* by David Hume
Timothy Ferriss: *Letters from a Stoic* by Seneca the Younger
Bill Gates: *Enlightenment Now* by Steven Pinker

Melinda Gates: *The Book of Awakening* by Mark Nepo
Malcolm Gladwell: *Just Kids* by Patti Smith
Jane Goodall: *The Story of Dr. Dolittle* by Hugh Lofting
Stephen Hawking: *Middlemarch* by George Eliot
Steve Jobs: *Autobiography of a Yogi* by Paramahansa Yogananda

Bruce Lee: The *Hero with a Thousand Faces* by Joseph Campbell
Abraham Lincoln: *Aesop's Fables*
Nelson Mandela: *War and Peace* by Leo Tolstoy
Gabriel García Márquez: *The Magic Mountain* by Thomas Mann
George R. R. Martin: *The Lord of the Rings* by J. R. R. Tolkien

Elon Musk: *The Hitchhiker's Guide to the Galaxy* by Douglas Adams
Trevor Noah: *The Little Prince* by Antoine de Saint-Exupéry
Bill Nye "The Science Guy": *The Physics of Baseball* by Robert Adair
Barack Obama: *The Broken Ladder* by Keith Payne
Michelle Obama: *Educated* by Tara Westover

Joe Rogan: *Food of the Gods* by Terence McKenna
J. K. Rowling: *Emma* by Jane Austen
Nikola Tesla: *Adventures of Huckleberry Finn* by Mark Twain
Emma Watson: *The Power* by Naomi Alderman
Oprah Winfrey: *The Bluest Eye* by Toni Morrison
Malala Yousafzai: *The Alchemist* by Paulo Coelho

Many of the above recommendations came from radicalreads.com, a site I recommend checking out if you would like more book recommendations from important and influential people.

Ultimately, it can be worth asking many people about their reading preferences if you want to seek out a wide repertoire of reading material. Ask questions such as "What is your favorite book?" "What is the most important book you ever read?" or "What is the book you read that impacted you the most?" You may ask a friend, your boss, a colleague, or someone who you happen to be sitting next to on a plane. You never know from who or where you will receive your next great book recommendation.

If you have not thought of it yet, start thinking about what book you would recommend to others that has had the deepest impact on you or that you think has been one of the most important books you have read.

Leaders Whose Book Recommendations are Worth Following

If you would like more book recommendations, here are some leaders who recommend many high-quality books that you may be interested in reading.

James Clear blogs about habits and human potential, helping to show us how we can live better lives. He is the author of *Atomic Habits*, which covers how to build good habits and break bad ones. Clear recommends both nonfiction and fiction books and focuses on personal development. The books he recommends often include topics such as art and creativity, biographies, business, fitness, history, philosophy, psychology, science, and writing. He also showcases a wide range of interests, recommending some classic novels, fantasy, and mystery books. Some of his top recommendations include *When Breath Becomes Air* by Paul Kalanithi, *Sapiens* by Yuval Noah Harari, and *Into Thin Air* by Jon Krakauer.

Bill Gates is the founder of Microsoft, co-founder of The Bill and Melinda Gates Foundation, and has signed the Giving Pledge – a pledge to give at least half of his wealth away through time. He also authored *Business @ the Speed of Thought*, which discusses how we can use technology to run better businesses. His book recommendations focus on nonfiction and big world issues that can impact us all. Common themes involve education, science, technology, self-development, business, history, and biographies. Gates' recommendations have often become personal favorites of mine. Some of his top recommendations include *Enlightenment Now* by Steven Pinker, *Measure What Matters* by John Doerr, and *Bad Blood* by John Carreyou.

Ryan Holiday is a writer and media strategist, and the founder of Brass Check, which has advised companies such as Google and many bestselling authors. His work often considers ancient philosophy and how we can use it to improve our lives today, which is a topic he explored in his book, *The Obstacle is the Way*. Holiday's recommendations tend toward nonfiction in topics such as philosophy, biographies, psychology, war and history. Some of his top recommendations include *Meditations* by Marcus Aurelius, *Letters from a Stoic* by Seneca, and *Man's Search for Meaning* by Viktor Frankl.

Emma Watson is an actress, model, and activist. She has promoted education for girls and in 2014 was appointed as a UN Women Goodwill ambassador. Watson has also launched a HeforShe campaign, where she has encouraged men to advocate for gender equality. Her book recommendations focus on women's issues, human issues, racism, sexism, inequality, and justice. Some of her top recommendations include *The Constant Princess* by Philippa Gregory, *A Thousand Splendid Suns* by Khaled Hosseini, and *The Handmaid's Tale* by Margaret Atwood.

Oprah Winfrey is a talk show host, actress, and philanthropist. She is best known for her talk show *The Oprah Winfrey Show* which ran for 25 years and was the most popular show of its type. She is also the author of *The Wisdom of Sundays,* which features some of the most meaningful and inspirational conversations she has had with thought-leaders. Winfrey's book recommendations focus on fiction, and often deal with themes such as discrimination and prejudice, life from the perspective of a diverse range of people, overcoming difficult life challenges, and the lives of women. Some of her top recommendations include *The Seat of the Soul* by Gary Zukav, *A Lesson Before Dying* by Ernest J. Gaines, and *Wild* by Cheryl Strayed.

Reese Witherspoon is an actress, producer, and entrepreneur. In 2016 she joined Otter Media to form Hello Sunshine, with the purpose of bringing more female-driven stories to film and TV. Witherspoon is also the author of *Whiskey in a Teacup,* about how growing up in the south impacted her whole life. Her recommendations focus on fiction, often from the female perspective, especially on overcoming challenges and female empowerment. A common theme is love, and she also enjoys thrillers and page-turners. Some of her recent recommendations include *The Secrets We Kept* by Lara Prescott, *The Cactus* by Sarah Haywood, and *From Scratch* by Tembi Locke.

Fareed Zakaria hosts Fareed Zakaria GPS for CNN Worldwide which focuses on international and US affairs, and he is a columnist for *The Washington Post.* Zakaria is also the author of *The Post-American World,* about the rising power of many nations around the world. He specializes in topics such as history, politics, government, the economy, and inequality, while he also recommends some books in personal development, business, psychology, philosophy, and literature. Recent recommendations include *The Song of Achilles* by Madeline Miller, *The Professor and the Madman* by Simon Winchester, and *Democracy and Dictatorship in Europe* by Sheri Berman.

With these recommendations from the above leaders and influencers, most of us should be able to find something new and insightful to read.

If you want further recommendations from the above individuals search their names and "book recommendations" or "book club" in your search engine. There are also many, many book bloggers online – you may find it useful to search for one who blogs about books in genres that interest you.

Pursue More Valuable Books

Perhaps you have seen a food pyramid, or a graphic that illustrated how some types of foods were better for you than others. There is a similar concept when it comes to reading. Not all books are created equal. Some types of books will be more worth reading than others, and our task is to find them.

In general, pursue more detailed books written by authorities on the topic that will teach you new insights, rather than on overly fluffy books that have only one insight and may result in you spending a lot of time reviewing concepts that are already obvious to you. Eventually if you are making advancements, you may read some books that are more academic in nature, or that are intended for people who already have expertise in a topic. These may be books that are marketed toward experts with many years of experience, a professional handbook, or they may even be textbooks intended for college students. Often there is one book or a few books in every industry that are viewed as required reading. If you aim to become an expert in a topic, you should acquire such books and read them thoroughly. Even if you are not ready to read these books yet, you can better prepare yourself for the task by familiarizing yourself with the topics that such keystone books cover.

Less valuable forms of reading will be fiction that is meant for quick disposable entertainment and which does not cover deeper themes, books that mostly cover sensational and trendy topics without prioritizing the truth, and books that present a superficial overview of other books or topics. Any reading that does not provoke thought, questions, help to build a greater understanding, or reveal something new to you, is generally a lower level of reading. You can still read such materials for fun, but these rarely provide much value to your life.

The most valuable books are the ones that are right for your specific circumstance. For example, if a family member has a rare illness and you want to help improve his condition, you may begin by reading general books on the illness, and then ones that are more specific, and eventually you may even pursue academic books or scientific articles to learn what the most cutting-edge research has to say. As an alternative, perhaps you want to make some extra money on the weekends to save up for a new car (or a used one). In that case, you would benefit from reading *Buy Buttons* by Nick Loper. Either way, you want to pursue those books which add value to your life, not those which simply drain your time.

Many people actually spend significant amounts of time reading – often through Google searches, texts, emails, advertisements, social media posts, celebrity news, or fashion magazines and blogs. This has an effect on your mind similar to what a junk food diet would have on your body. It does not provide much value or nourishment. We would be better served to read in topics such as science, technology, history, self-development, biographies, philosophy, and literature with deep and complex themes. I would urge you to read books that challenge you to grow in your knowledge, understanding, intellect, and emotional or spiritual growth. Limit the "junk food" forms of reading and replace them with quality reads.

What Types of Books will Help to Become a More Insightful Reader and Thinker?

Distinguishing between Fact and Fiction

Some topics that could be beneficial for developing your critical thinking and reading skills are books on logic and logical fallacies, persuasion, and cognitive biases. Learning about logic and logical fallacies will help you with understanding whether the points in a book are reasonable and logically follow based on the author's premises. Learning about persuasion will help you to realize when a book is using persuasive techniques to convince you of something rather than offering true substance. For a useful book on persuasion, see *Thank You for Arguing* by Jay Heinrichs. The next theme you should learn about is cognitive biases, which will help you to see common thinking traps that the author can fall into, which make their points sound legitimate, but may actually not be sound at all. Notice that the general theme here is that you should focus on learning about topics that help you to see what is real and what is not when you read. Not every word you read will be based in reality – and you must develop your skills to differentiate between fact and fiction.

Philosophy and Questioning

Reading some philosophy can also help your critical thinking and reading skills, as philosophy is largely about asking questions about the world around us, and in order to be a good reader, you have to keep asking questions. You cannot passively accept everything that the author has told you. A skilled reader should always be thinking: *What if instead of what the author says, we tried something else? Does what the author says apply in all circumstances – more importantly, does it apply in my case? Is what the author says a hard rule or just a soft recommendation? The author assumes this to be the case, but what if his basic assumption is wrong?* To help inspire you to ask more questions, you may wish to start a journal of your own questions that you acquire from your readings or from life itself. Then when you have time, you can pursue your own answers to your questions, likely through reading.

The Intersection of Topics

To expand your knowledge and reading abilities, read books that intersect with many different topics. For this, I would urge you to read biographies, as biographies are told in the form of captivating stories and will also intersect with many other topics such as history, self-improvement and life lessons, scientific advancements, ethical issues, personal traumas, and so forth. Also, make a note of books that combine themes that interest you. For example, *A History of the World in 6 Glasses* by Tom Standage combines history and beverages (e.g., water, beer, coffee, wine), *Ten Things Video Games Can Teach Us* by Jordan Erica Webber and Daniel Griliopoulos combines video games and philosophy, and *Extreme Ownership* by Jocko Willink combines elite military forces (e.g., US Navy Seals) with corporate leadership. Books that intersect with two or more topics will be highly valuable, as you can improve in your understanding of many different themes all at once.

Classical and often mentioned books

Some books are referred to or mentioned over and over in conversations, classrooms, and in other books because they are considered to be classics. These classical books are referred to often enough that if you read some of them it will help advance your reading abilities. This is because you will be able to more deeply understand the discussions of more modern authors, which are often based on or influenced by classical works. Here are some examples of classical books that can help you to become a sharper reader and thinker, if you were to read them deeply: Various religious books such as the Bible, Shakespeare's works, *Aesop's Fables*, *Grimm's Tales*, *The Illiad* and *The Odyssey* by Homer, *The Art of War* by Sun Tzu, *The Republic* by Plato, *Don Quixote* by Miguel de Cervantes, *Divine Comedy* by Dante Alighieri, *The Library of Apollodorus* by Apollodorus of Athens, *Histories* by Herodotus, and *The Prince* by Niccolo Machiavelli. Many modern books may assume that you have already read some of these older works, or they may be inspired by them. If in your readings you often see that a particular book is cited, then that book is likely one you should add to your "to reads" list, as it will be a foundational book that can aid in your understanding of both older and more modern works.

Get Clues From Your Favorite Books

Remember that you can always type your favorite book titles into book sites (e.g., Amazon or Goodreads) and see what other recommendations come up in lists that they may call "Also bought" or "Readers also enjoyed." These books are recommended based on the sites' algorithms, depending on the books that other readers tended to buy or read together.

You can also carefully read through your favorite books and make a note of any books that are mentioned inside that you think could be interesting. If you especially appreciate an author, any other books he mentions are likely to be possible new favorites of yours too. Such books will likely provide more detail or context on the original book's topic.

Often, it helps to check if there is a list at the end of your favorite books, of references or further readings. Such lists can provide a good starting point to help you figure out what to read next.

Seek Out Books with Characters or Themes That Speak to You

If you are a loner, you may look for books with outsiders and lone wolves as the heroes. If you are into video games, you may seek out books that take place in a video game world. Or if you are into fashion, you may seek books that have characters who are obsessed with being fashionable or who work in the fashion industry. These tips are especially useful if you find that you often choose books where you do not relate to the author or characters and you do not understand why they care about the things that they do. When this happens, you may need to pursue a more personal connection in your readings. Think of the author or main characters as friends that you get to choose. Pursuing books that you have a strong common ground with can be a starting point, but in time I recommend moving away from books that focus solely on the roles that you normally associate with, to help expand your horizons.

Look for stories that inspire and excite you – do not feel compelled to read what everyone else is reading or what the well-read experts say you should read if you find that you do not tend to enjoy such books or find them useful. One of the greatest points to remember is to have fun. Perhaps you want to learn history, but most historical accounts are too dry for you. Then start with historical fiction to get a taste of what an era was like. Or read a book of fascinating and unconventional historical stories, rather than a dry and academic text. If you need visuals to appreciate scientific concepts, then browse an encyclopedia or a book with some illustrations such as *The Illustrated Brief History of Time* by Stephen Hawking.

Filter Out the Books That Are Not Worth Reading

There are so many books to read that I have developed my own system for filtering out the ones that are not likely to be useful to me. Here are the criteria that I consider before buying or reading a book. You can focus on the ones which are most useful to you.

Check the title and cover

Does the cover grab your interest? Is the title in a topic that you are curious about? Can you get a grasp of the genre and the general idea that this book will cover? Does the cover look polished and professional? The cover is the first impression you get about a book, and it makes sense to consider this first in deciding whether you are interested in reading it. I am pickier with how I assess newer books. For the older classics, I am not going to worry about whether the title or cover capture my interest, as they have already been recognized as worthy reads.

Check reviews

You may wish to choose a certain review rating where you will not read books below that level. I would not set it too high because you can eliminate some very good books if you do that. But it can be useful as a general filter, to avoid wasting your time on bad books. For example, if a book is rated below 3.5, I may decide not to read the book just based on this rating. I do not set the criteria at 4.0 or higher because there are actually many great books that fall below that standard. I recommend choosing a rating from 3.5 – 3.8 as your criteria, where you will not read books below such a rating unless it comes highly recommended. Conversely, there are many books that are not especially noteworthy with near perfect reviews, so do not rely on *just* the numerical rating to decide what to read.

If a book seems like it will require a big investment of my time or money, perhaps if it is long, highly advanced, or expensive, then I like to read some reviews to see if buying the book is likely to pay off. Of course, if the book is fiction, I may just read one or two reviews to avoid spoiling the whole book – or if I am worried about getting too much information and ruining it, I may only read the description to get a general overview and then make my decision. I like to read reviews to get an idea about whether a book is worth reading, but I would be cautious with relying too much on what the reviewers say – there will always be critics, even for the best books of all time. Keep in mind that some fiction books may have bad character development and even bad story-telling, but they may have some truly deep and thought-provoking insights that make it worthwhile. It would be a pity to read a few bad reviews and then be swayed away from reading such a valuable book. In the end, remember that all books suffer from limitations, as there is no such thing as the perfect book.

What year was this published?

I like to check the year that the book was published to have an idea of what to expect. You can find this in the online description of the book, or in the first few pages on the copyright page. For books that involve scientific or technological topics, I usually prefer for them to have been published within the prior five years. On the other hand, if I were interested in learning about the formation of Walmart as a company, I may seek older books that were written closer to that time period for a realistic portrayal of what was happening at that time. For events in history, I may read books that were written close to the time period that I am interested in, if I want the perspective of someone who lived through it. Or I may read a book that was written many years or decades afterward, if I want a wider perspective that can better explain why events happened as they did.

Keep in mind that if we go back many decades, or hundreds of years to much older publications, authors tended to write in different styles that can seem unusual or outdated. If this bothers you, you may avoid much older books.

As a final point, be aware that very old but popular books are often reprinted or republished, so you may see a thousand-year-old book that shows 2015 as the publication date. This typically means that the book has a new cover, a new translation, or that a new introduction or illustrations have been added. Older editions are usually more faithful to the original words used, while more recent editions are usually easier to read.

A pamphlet, a book, or a tome?

Now, let us consider what page count you are looking for in a book. Perhaps you are wondering why I would bother to mention this. The size should not be that important, right? If you believe that a book has many brilliant insights, whether it is 200 or 400 pages should not make much of a difference, you would assume. Generally, I agree with this idea. However, the issue is that with eBooks, some authors will publish books anywhere from 10-50 pages, which is much lower than you would normally expect. Also, although it is less common, if an eBook is 1,000 pages, you may be surprised to realize this after purchasing it, and not be eager to invest quite that much time into learning the material. The point here is for eBook readers especially – check the page count early on to avoid wasting your time. If a book is far outside of the range you prefer, look for another book. There is nothing wrong with a 20-page book, as there is nothing wrong with a 2,000-page book, as long as the reader understands that this is what he is purchasing. You will find that with eBooks, the only way to know the page count is by searching for it in the descriptive information provided about the book online.

Check out more details – the book description, table of contents, and the "look inside" or sample feature

If you have checked the above criteria and you are still interested, then you should read the book's description to get a better idea of what topics it will cover, and what key questions or information it will focus on. It is also a good idea to flip to the table of contents to see if some of these topics interest you. This is important because sometimes a book's title is meant to capture attention, and then when you begin reading, you find that the book does not cover what you expected at all. If that is the case, you may discover this more quickly by browsing the table of contents. Assuming you are still interested in the book, you can read some of the introduction, and possibly even the conclusion (if you are holding a paperback) to see what direction the book is going in. Even for eBooks, many sites allow you to see the beginning part of the book (e.g., a "look inside" or sample feature) to help you decide if you would like to read it in full. I recommend taking advantage of this to avoid spending money on a book that did not truly interest you. This is a phase of getting to know the book before committing to it fully.

Who is the author?

Something else to consider is who your author is, and what their expertise is on a topic. To learn about the author, you may find a section for this on the book's page online, or sometimes you can learn more about your author by clicking on a link of their name, which is also on the book's page. Generally, I want an author who takes his or her topic seriously, but she does not necessarily need to have a specific background for me to buy her book. Of course, for highly technical or advanced topics, I prefer to see some formal credentials or many years of experience. As an example, if an author writes 10 books focused on how to make money, and she owns multiple profitable businesses, I would happily purchase this type of book from her. However, I would probably not read a book about physics from her, unless I had a reason to believe that she was also an expert in this field.

Take a Chance on New Books

I encourage you to view books as vessels of knowledge and wisdom that are worth taking a chance on. I used to be quite picky about what I would read. When I was in a bookstore, I would study the front and back of a book carefully, then I would read the introduction and the author biography, and often I still would not be sure if I wanted to read it. Ultimately, I would not purchase the book and leave the store empty-handed. In the past several years, I have been more inclined to take a chance on books that caught my interest in some way – even if I was not sure. Of course, sometimes the reasons for choosing a book can be superficial, as I may be captivated by an interesting cover or catchy title, and it is always possible that the quality is subpar. But in general books are not very expensive, so if the price is not too steep then it may be worth taking a chance on.

Remember that all it takes is one amazing point, insight, or story to change everything around for you. Conceivably, any book could provide this, suggesting that sometimes you should take a chance and check out a book even if you are not sure about it. Another way to take a chance is to pick up books that you do not feel you would normally read, but that still interest you in some way. Perhaps you do not normally read Western novels, but you find one that has deep philosophical themes and you love philosophy. This may be a good book to take a chance on. Books are like little experiments – perhaps your choice will pay off big. Even if it does not, you will likely learn something about the types of books you should avoid in the future. Essentially, if you think a book could be filled with nuggets of knowledge and wisdom, then you do not have much to lose with reading it.

If you want to let loose and take chances on new and different types of books, you can visit a library or sign up to a subscription service (e.g., Scribd or Kindle Unlimited) where you can download any number of books for a set monthly price. Since you are not paying for individual books, you will not feel the need to finish every single one you start. You may take a chance on a book, decide it is not worth it, then move on to the next one.

Read Basic and Summary Books or Elaborate Ones?

Books that summarize complex ideas into very short summaries tend to be more and more popular as time passes. For example, you can find books that summarize all of philosophy, psychology, or even physics. *For Dummies* and *A Very Short Introduction* are examples of this type of series. These books can be useful depending on your goals, but we should remember that there is a lot of value in reading works which are tougher to read, denser, and more elaborate as well. Earlier in your reading journey it could make sense to read some of these summary books to get a rough overview of different domains. But soon enough you will outgrow them, and you will feel yourself yearning for much more detail. Keep in mind that an important topic or person in history is not always easily summarized within a few pages – the real story is often in the details that you must explore more deeply. The best use of summary books may be if they spark a desire in you to learn more, and to read more deeply in certain topics. If you want to sample a new topic that you know little about, these summary books can be a start. My main critique is that some of these books over-summarize, breaking down complex ideas into a single sentence or failing to include important background information, and the content can become quite superficial at that point.

When you read a book with extremely simple points, without a deeper substance to them, you will be more likely to forget the material quite easily. This means that often the books that oversimplify and over-summarize will have limited use, as you will lack complete understanding and the ability to apply what you learned. My advice: Use summary books as a doorway into deeper themes, not as a way to avoid them.

Reading

An Introduction

Now that we have discussed how to find good books to read, you are ready to begin reading. This is the easy part, right? You have been reading all of your life, so you know what to do. Well, yes and no. When we are kids, we learn to read but we do not put much effort in advancing our reading skills beyond a basic level. Typically, this means that we focus on *what* has happened on the pages, instead of truly examining *why* or *how* it happened, or what the implications are, or why it even matters. As adults, many of us will continue this pattern of reading superficially.

An insight I gained from reading *Moonwalking with Einstein* by Joshua Foer is that **people quickly reach a plateau in their learning where they stop improving. This is because we reach a point that is "good enough," and we do not push ourselves to improve after this.** The mind tends to become lazy after you have learned to do something to a point that is good enough to get by. An example would be driving. Most people know how to drive, but all you have to do is look at people's driving skills on the road to see that we are not close to optimizing our abilities. People drive while distracted, and they do not have any process for looking for faster routes, typically taking the same routes whether they are best or not. They may not have learned how to properly drive in different weather conditions such as on icy roads or in fog, or how to parallel park, despite many years of driving experience. Many of us will not improve at all in our skills after having acquired around 5-10 years of experience driving. The same thing may be true for reading, where we do not advance much after we have been reading for perhaps 5-10 years. We get used to reading the usual types of books that we read, in our usual way, and never advance much in our abilities, despite that we have the potential to do so. This is not something we should be satisfied with. *We should do something about this, don't you think? The real question is: what can we do about it?*

First, we must realize that the brain naturally becomes lazy and reluctant to grow when we have become good enough, and we must fight this mindset if we wish to keep improving as individuals.

In this section we will discuss how you can continue to improve in your reading abilities, even if you have been unable to make progress in a long time. Much of this section will have to do with keeping a focused mind as you read. The mind without focus will tend to read passively and remember and understand less. To read well and gain the most from your readings, you must learn to *activate your mind.*

Read and Learn Efficiently

Most of us assume that we should read our books from start to finish. As a general tendency, I do this, but you may wish to experiment with how you read as this is not always the most efficient way to proceed.

Occasionally, I will buy a book and there will be multiple sections of the book that do not apply to me at all. There will be full sections where I have no reason to read them. As an example, let's say you are reading a book about improving your relationship. Then let's say that the first chapter is an introductory overview about why relationships are important. It is short, so you read it. Then the first full chapter is about finding that perfect partner for you. However, you are already in a happy relationship (in this theoretical scenario at least), so the section does not apply to you. You would be best off in simply skipping the section. When you already know the information, or when it does not apply to you, it is better to skip. This may feel strange at first, but to read information that is of no value is just wasting your time.

Another reason you may skip a section is if it does not hold your interest, but most of the rest of the book does. If a section truly does not interest you and it bores you and is not important to understanding the book, you may move on to the next section. Also, consider that if you have a background or contextual information in a topic, you may sometimes sense that you already know the argument the author is going to make, and you have no need to read it. It is like when a friend starts telling a story you have heard before (to someone else in your group) – you feel no need to listen because you already know where he is going with this. In the end, there is little point in forcing yourself to get through something you will gain little benefit from.

You may also choose to skip a section when the material is simply too advanced and it goes into an area that will be highly difficult for you to understand, and likely with limited benefit. For example, a physics book may start off simply, and gradually get to extremely theoretical ideas that are difficult to grasp and possibly throw in equations that you struggle to comprehend. It may be best to avoid the most advanced sections of such a text if you do not think they will provide much benefit for your specific needs. Of course, if you are a physicist or plan to become one, you should make an effort to understand such a challenging section even if it is difficult to follow. For a layperson, however, you may spend your time better by learning something else.

Another key instance when you may skip chapters is when you have a very specific purpose for reading, such as with *surgical reading*, and you need the information now, where you lack the time and interest to read a full book. Let's imagine a computer engineer who needs to solve a problem with his computer code on a program he is working on. Even with all of his expertise, he is still unable to figure out the solution on his own. He is not interested in learning all of the theory about *why* something may or may not work – he wants to resolve this specific problem. After researching the problem, he finds a book that covers his particular issue in detail, so this is a great start. In the introduction, the author discusses why this problem is important and why it is common and how it can be quite difficult to resolve, but the engineer does not care about this introductory material. He wants solutions now, so he skips it. Then the book discusses common scenarios where this problem tends to occur. He flips to the table of contents and headings to get an idea of where the author is going, and he realizes that he already tried most of the solutions that the book proposes.

Finally, toward the end of the book, the author discusses uncommon reasons for having issues with the code and there are 7 key points. The engineer runs through these proposed solutions one by one, following the directions carefully in efforts to fix his code. On point 3, he manages to resolve his problem. Rather than reading the whole book to fix the issue, he spent 15 minutes on it. He used the book as a tool to fix his specific problem with surgical precision, managing to get maximum value in the minimum time.

With some books, if you are interested in specific segments rather than the book as a whole, you may pay significant attention to the table of contents, reading the book according to your points of interest rather than all of it. This may make sense for a very large book. For example, I recently read Bruce Lee's and Leonardo da Vinci's biographies in this way, focusing on specific periods of their lives that I found more interesting. I am fascinated by such people's lives, but I often struggle to read a full biography of 600+ pages straight through. Sometimes I prefer to find periods that I relate to in their lives, or that I think are the most interesting and read only those parts. This type of tip also makes sense for other very long or encyclopedic books. Perhaps you are reading a book that discusses a hundred important figures in history (e.g., *The 100* by Michael Hart). In that case, you may not feel the need to read the book from beginning to end, but instead focus on the people who capture your attention the most, flipping through the book using the table of contents as your guide.

If you are reading a technical, information dense, or academic book, be sure to make use of the index (usually in the back of the book). If you are looking for something such as a key term or a person or principle, you are likely to find this in the index and then you can learn precisely this, rather than wasting time on unnecessary information. This feature of books is probably not used as often as it should be, and it saves a lot of time. If you are reading an eBook, you can search for technical words or terms quite easily – as usually there is a search feature built into your e-reader or e-reading app.

What if you do not want to read a book in the supposedly most efficient way, and you simply want to enjoy reading it in the traditional way? This is perfectly fine too. If you are reading a book where you are fascinated with the material, or where you want to learn everything as deeply as possible without missing anything, where you truly respect the author and want to absorb it all, then by all means read the book from front to back without skipping anything. When I want to learn something as deeply as possible, I will do this. Sometimes the author will elaborate more than is needed, reviewing points you are already familiar with, and sometimes the author will have a conclusion that repeats points that you already understood. But there can be a value to **overlearning –** which means to continue to learn or practice something even after you have already become proficient. This can help to make sure that you fully understand everything and that you are fully prepared to apply the information in your life. Some people may think they know something and that they do not need a review – but remember what was mentioned earlier – *easy learning means easy forgetting.* If things are too clear and obvious with little effort on your part, perhaps you did not truly understand it, and perhaps it will be easily forgotten. I tend to spend more attention on finding good books to read with many insights, and then I read them thoroughly. Many people will assume they know what the author is going to say based on his premises, but unless you read everything carefully, you may be making mistaken assumptions. Perhaps the author will delve into greater complexities than you had originally expected.

In discussing efficiency and pacing, I feel the need to mention speed reading. I believe that it is a mistake of modern society that we are too obsessed with speed. I think it is more important to read deeply than speedily. We are living in a society that wants to do everything quickly without actually thinking about what we are doing. We are so outcome-focused that we overlook the process or system that it takes to get to those desired outcomes. We all want shortcuts, but the truly successful people I am aware of did not try to shortcut the system. When you look too hard for shortcuts at the expense of quality, then you end up with lackluster results. These are my opinions, but you are more than welcome to experiment with speed reading, and to experiment with my systems for reading. Perhaps you will find that both are useful in different circumstances. The bottom line is to make sure that you are learning, absorbing, and understanding so that you can acquire insights from your readings. Then you can apply what you learn to improve your life or the lives of those around you – this is what truly matters, not the pace with which you finish a book, and not the number of books that you have read.

Ask Questions as You Read

Why are you reading? This is a key question that you must always keep in mind. What is your objective? What is it that you want to accomplish? When you have your objective, ask supporting questions that you expect the book to answer. If your objective is to learn how to change careers, then other sub-questions you may have are – *How do I leave my current job without upsetting my employers? How much notice do I need to give when leaving my job? How can I learn everything I need to learn for my new career in the shortest time?* If you find a book on changing careers, but do not see the answers to these types of questions, then you should look for another book until you find one that does answer your specific questions.

Some other questions you may ask are: *What is the thesis or main idea of this book? Do the assumptions made by the author make sense? Does one statement logically lead to the next, and do the conclusions follow from the premises stated? Is the author consistent in what he says?* If he contradicts himself, this is not internally consistent and means there is likely a mistake somewhere in his reasoning. Be cautious with assuming that all of the author's statements logically flow. When he states his facts, consider them carefully. Do those facts match up with what you have seen and experienced and read elsewhere, or is there a conflict? Be aware that if his facts and arguments are dubious, then his conclusions will be dubious.

If a book is based on personal experience, then if the author had a very different background or upbringing than you, it is quite likely that he will be working with different assumptions, and those assumptions will lead him to different conclusions than what you would have reached. Such books can help you to gain a different perspective, but ultimately you may find yourself disagreeing with some of the assumptions and therefore some of the conclusions. For more technical and advanced books, you may find yourself relying on the learned community to see if the logic is sound. For example, if you are learning about thermodynamics or the laws of motion and you are not an expert in physics, you may not feel that you are in the position to question the logic of such principles. In that case, you must rely on the experiments and reasoning of the people who are reputable in the field.

When you are a beginner it does make sense to trust the logic and reasoning of those who are more advanced, but as you become more advanced yourself, you should aim to think more critically about the logical flow of ideas, and not take it for granted that something is logical just because someone smarter or with more education said so. I recommend that you start questioning right away – even if you do not feel ready. As ridiculous as it may feel to question an established principle – questioning it will only turn you into a brighter student who understands much more deeply, rather than being someone who memorizes ideas without understanding. Do not be afraid to question grand principles, even if it makes you feel silly – for example, you may ask: *Is gravity a real phenomenon? Is there a better way to govern than the major systems that have been used up to now (e.g., democracy, monarchy, dictatorship, etc.)? Did the Big Bang really happen? Is the scientific method truly the best way to discover truths?* Asking questions and then remaining ignorant would not be a great feat, of course, but if you question and dig deeper into the material, then you will have a much more fruitful learning experience than someone who did not ask questions.

A central question to keep in mind is: *Is what I am reading true?* Many people pick up a nonfiction book thinking they are reading to learn and to understand, but they quickly get sidetracked by the sensational, gossip, shocking words or scenarios, amazing and extravagant claims, and intense narratives with good and evil and heroes and villains. And in getting caught up in all of this, they lose track of the truth. They get distracted and stop analyzing critically, enthralled in what the words are saying. Yes, it is interesting when an author dazzles us with his words as if he were pulling off a magic trick of sorts, keeping us hanging on to every word – but the fundamental questions are: *Is this true? Is this real? Is this valuable?* Do not forget it.

The mind naturally fixates on grand and extravagant stories. But a well-crafted story does not make something true. Our minds operate as story-building machines. We can turn any sequence of events into a story, but perhaps the story we have crafted is not fully true. Perhaps it is the way our minds work. Our minds are attracted to action and drama, and loss or death as such events are usually important to our lives. We build stories to make sense of things, and our stories tend to reflect the reality in some way, but perhaps the story is just a convenient one. The ancient Greeks for example had Poseidon, god of the sea. He was the reason for the tides and oceanic storms – but to us, this is just silliness. Gravity, meteorology, and science explain these phenomena for us now. Here we see that stories are often simpler and easier to remember, with direct causes and effects, but sometimes the reality is much more complex than the stories would have us believe.

To find truth, ask yourself what evidence the book provides. Is it based on personal experience? Scientific research? Reading deeply? Logic and reason? Or is it conjecture and speculation? Does the author make it clear what type of evidence the book is based on, or are you left guessing? You have to have an idea of what level of truth the information reaches. However, something to consider is that regardless of how truthful the information is, your personal truth may be different. For example, if a study says that 90% of people in your neighborhood did not graduate from a university, this is not any proof or evidence about whether *you* graduated, or your capabilities for doing so.

Ask yourself when reading: *Is this true now? Will this be true in the future? Was this true in the past? Does increasing awareness of a truth somehow make it less likely to be true in the future?* For example, let's imagine that there is a popular article that says yellow is the magic color used in advertisements that makes most people buy products. Then the ad agencies read this and make *all* their ads yellow. In time, almost all ads become yellow, and the color ceases to have any effect because it is overused and people no longer like it. Yellow being the magic color that sells would be something that was true at one point or in one situation, but which was not universally true in all situations. Many, many so-called truths operate in this way, which is probably why people often get into heated debates with one another. Many things are true in some cases and not others. And to make things more complex, people being aware of a "truth" can make it stop being true (as in the example above with the color yellow).

The Pursuit of Truth

In truth, truth is a tricky subject. New scientific studies often provide us with evidence that casts into doubt what we thought we knew or that even proves we were wrong. To me, proof is never final – it is just overwhelming evidence in support of something. But in a sense, everything in our world is a matter of belief, because even our most firm systems of thinking and understanding could be wrong. Something that happens a million times in a row such as the sun rising and setting is likely to happen another million times, but this does not apply forever. One day (e.g., in billions of years), the sun will no longer exist in its current form, and cease to rise and fall thereafter. No rule or principle is infallible, applying 100% of the time. Thus, perhaps we simply have not acquired sufficient evidence to prove certain things wrong, *yet*.

An interesting idea that some very smart people such as Elon Musk (e.g., founder of SpaceX and co-founder of Tesla) have entertained is that we may be living inside a simulated reality, rather than the true base reality. This would mean that we are not true living beings, but rather a sort of complex robot that thinks it is alive. Even if this is the case, there may be no way for us know for sure. Unfortunately, certain things cannot be proven or disproven either way: we simply lack the evidence and the ability to test for it. In such cases, we may need to create our own personal truth, which is what we choose to believe.

We all have our own versions of what is true for us. This is the reason that it can be fascinating to read different perspectives on the same topic. For example, read three different accounts of what happened in the Vietnam war from three different soldiers, and you may get wildly different accounts. However, the truth of any one soldier does not invalidate the truth of any other soldier.

The typical modern understanding of truth is that scientific research provides us with the highest truth, but in my opinion, anecdotal information (e.g., from personal experiences) can be highly worthwhile too and is not something that should be easily discounted. Science studies what is happening in the real world, in a seemingly objective way, but we are creatures with subjective viewpoints experiencing the world, who are doing the research in a quest to discover objective truths. However, we are not able to access the real world in its full complexity through our subjective experiences. Just because my senses, mind, or instruments allow me to perceive the world in a certain way, does not mean that I am perceiving the absolute truth. For example, are there more dimensions than we can perceive, and are those dimensions able to impact us in ways that we are not aware of? Perhaps science is the most powerful framework we have to identify truth in areas where variables can conveniently be observed, isolated, examined, and turned into data which can be meaningfully analyzed and interpreted, but even this form of pursuing truth has its limitations.

Keep in mind that scientific studies and their results are sometimes reflective of the truth. Likewise, anecdotal or intuitive experiences are sometimes reflective of the truth. Science may be more accurate overall, since it is able to examine large collections of data to identify the patterns that likely correspond to our reality. However, often our subjective experiences cannot be *properly* studied in a scientific way. As an example, we *cannot* study your feelings scientifically, but we can study what you report your feelings to be. Of course, your report may be inaccurate if you are repressing your feelings, unaware of them, or unable to describe them. These are the limitations of attempting to study the subjective experience.

In essence, no one has all the answers: neither science, nor our subjective and personal experiences. Neither numerical data nor our human senses, intuition, and reasoning fully capture the world that we live in. We do not have any one process for determining what is absolutely true with absolute certainty. Use every resource available to you – your anecdotal experience, your senses, your mental acuity, your logic and creativity, science, speculations in the books you read, religion and spirituality, and so forth. Intermingle it all in your own mind to create your own special cocktail of truth. Do not limit yourself to one particular viewpoint. If we all look at things the same way, under the same framework, then we are just limiting the truths that we are capable of accessing.

The question that matters most when it comes to truth is whether your personal truth syncs with the truth that the author is writing about. Assume that the author is making her best faith effort to speak truth, but that it is possible that her truth simply diverges too greatly from your own truth. As a basic example, *if* I believe that life is wonderful because everyone I have known has become my friend and treated me well and loved me, but your life experience has been completely in contradiction, then we have diverging truths, but both experiences are true. However, it is clear that a book on the wonderfulness of life may be of limited value if you find yourself in horrible circumstances which have been there for all of your existence. Do not assume that the author is wrong or deceitful – perhaps her truth is simply different than yours.

How to Handle Strange Facts

When I come across strange facts that do not sound right, I like to look them up. I once read a book on philosophy that stated as a fact that humans were made up of *millions* of cells. I do not have a background in biology, but I like to read general science articles and books, and I was surprised that the number would be so low. I looked it up, and humans actually have about 37 *trillion* cells. Apparently, the idea of "millions" is so far off as to be laughable, as a million times a million is a trillion, meaning that the figure of "millions of cells" is about a million times away from the reality. Of course, this was not a science book, it was a philosophy book. And the error was not stated as a central argument of the book, instead it was stated to help the author make one particular point. Mistakes will be made, as humans are imperfect, and in a full book of hundreds of facts, perhaps we can give an author a break for having one incorrect piece of information.

As a reading exercise, assume that each book you read has at least one mistake in it, and you will keep a more alert mind that way. Notice that the more prior knowledge you bring with you as you read a book, the more likely you are to catch such errors in your readings.

Fortunately, the error mentioned above did not have much effect on my understanding of the book, since the "fact" was not important to the overall message. The most critical facts in a book of course will be those which are central to the book's arguments. If I write a book about how my favorite phone is the iPhone because it is one of the cheapest on the market, and my purpose in writing is to convince you to buy an iPhone, then clearly we have a problem. In case you are not aware, the iPhone is likely the most expensive phone on the market, not the cheapest. If you find such glaring mistakes, I would recommend looking for another book. Clearly, this type of mistake should not happen if the book is written by an expert.

As you read and come across strange facts or potential errors, ask questions such as: *Is this really true? What is the evidence for this? Would most experts agree with this statement? Did this actually happen in this time period? Is the author exaggerating?* My advice: Question deeply, but with an open mind. Ask questions and seek your own answers. The book is merely a tool, it is a version of the truth, and not the complete and total truth.

Taking Action

Ideally, you will read and take action based on what you read, then you will read something new based on the results of the actions you took. If you find that what you originally read helped you greatly and solved all your problems, you may be ready to switch topics and investigate a new area that you would like to improve in. Alternatively, if you read, then take action, then are disappointed that your actions did not have the results you would have expected, then you can choose to continue trying more of the suggestions from your book, or you can choose to look for new books that may provide you with better guidance. Also recognize that it is always possible that you misapplied what you read. Perhaps you need to reread a section to make sure you fully understood it.

Even though reading is hugely beneficial, I firmly believe that life is meant to be lived. I think the best life is one that involves reading, thinking, and taking action. We need to act on what we read and learn, otherwise the information and insights will not do us much good. What use is it to have a critical piece of knowledge and then to do nothing about it?

Ultimately you will need to decide how much time to spend reading, and how much to spend taking action. In general, if you are dealing with a pivotal moment in your life where there is a major problem or situation, then you should read as deeply as you can before taking actions that could lead you down completely different paths. If you are in a situation where the costs would be immense for making any mistakes, again read deeply. I have heard many times from business professionals that if they had known just one key piece of information, it would have saved them a large sum of money. When a lot of money or time is at stake, or possibly human lives, then I would recommend reading quite deeply about the topic of interest if time permits. On the other hand, if there is not much of anything to lose from taking action and experimenting, you may read and take action around the same time if you prefer. For example, when reading about how to write your own song lyrics, you may experiment with writing songs while reading about the topic. You do not necessarily need to finish reading a book or any number of books in order to begin writing your own songs, since there is not much at risk here.

Social Service

As you read, think about who you can help with the insights that you are learning. Is there someone who *needs* to read the book you are reading? If you know people who rarely read or do not read at all though, do not try to force it upon them. Instead, share your deep insights from what you read and try to help them. Make sure to let them know what book you got the insight from in case they want to read it. If you would like, you can even offer to lend or give them a copy of the book.

Intending to help others will ultimately benefit your understanding of the material, as you will be keeping in mind how it can be applied. Remember that recalling random facts is generally not a good use of your time. You will be much better off in recalling patterns of facts that somehow support insights, narratives, your social network, or specific actions you want to take.

Even if you aim to help yourself through your readings, you can accomplish this more efficiently if you think of others. Conversely, if you wish to help others, you can often use that knowledge to help yourself as well.

Do not Be Afraid to Feel Something About What You Read

Have you ever gotten into an argument with an author, even if the argument just took place in your own mind while you were reading? Do not worry if it has. Even though we are discussing books here, these kinds of arguments can be helpful for your learning. Feel free to ask the author (at least in your head), *how dare you write this,* or *how dare you make claims without any evidence.* Feel open to criticize and critique the author and tell him what you really feel about his writing. For your learning, you do not need to passively agree with everything the author says, or with the logic of his arguments, or anything he writes. It is okay to disagree, to form more and more questions, wondering if anything he says is actually accurate.

You *should* find problems with his thinking, facts, reasoning, motives, and so forth. You should, because it is very difficult to say or write anything that is 100% accurate, 100% of the time. Reality is too complex for this. There will be many flaws to find, and the more you practice good reading habits, the more you will tend to find those flaws. To find more of these errors – first assume that they are there. *Assume* that the author made mistakes in his logic, thinking, facts, and conclusions. As strange as this seems, this is the key way that you will find such mistakes. Many people believe that if a book has faulty thinking, premises, or conclusions then it is not worth reading. This is not necessarily the case. I have learned a great deal from some books that I ultimately disagreed with or that I discovered flaws in. Some books cause you to think deeply about what you truly think and believe, and this can be hugely valuable even if you disagree with its conclusions. Another benefit of some of these flawed books is that you get to exercise your skills for finding faults in your readings. It is important that you build this skill set to become a more critical reader and thinker.

If you feel especially strongly about a book, I may even recommend an exercise of writing the author a note with everything that was wrong (or perhaps right) about the book and what you would have hoped to read instead. (I do not actually recommend sending such a note, unless you can make it constructive and include positive feedback as well.)

Then based on your critique, seek out new books to read that will help you meet your goals. Every book has the potential to benefit you, even some of those with glaring flaws. Do not get too frustrated with the bad or unhelpful books that you read, and instead allow them to guide you closer to the books that you should be reading. In this way you will always be making progress in your reading, learning, and personal goals.

As you continue in your reading journey, at some point you may feel outrage at certain injustices. This is a normal progression – as you learn more, you will see that not everything is as it should be. You may think, *How could we let this happen? Why have things gotten so bad and no one seems to be doing anything about it?* In such cases, you can form more and more questions, and fuel a deeper and deeper interest in certain topics. Then, you can use your curiosity and discontentedness to figure out what to read next. Continue reading more about the issues that concern you until you truly understand them. Through deeper learning, you will feel prepared to take action and become a part of the solution yourself.

What if the Book Does Not Resonate with You?

Some people feel like they must finish every book they start. Bill Gates, a very smart and accomplished man (and wealthiest person in the world for 18 years, nonconsecutively) has this habit of finishing every book he starts. Although this approach may work for him, I do not think it is the optimal way to read. Sometimes the book simply is not a good fit for your needs. Perhaps you are reading a book and your mind is completely at odds with everything in it. The author may be overly rational and logical, but your brain is more wired for stories and emotion and excitement, or vice versa. Maybe the book is influenced by a cultural or religious background that you struggle to relate to. It does not help you much if you force yourself to read a book that is not of any interest or value to you. If you are not engaged with a book, set it aside. Then, search for one that will better help you to meet your objectives and be interesting for you at the same time.

I would recommend separating the books that you abandon into different types. Do not lump them all into one pile. You may choose to abandon some books permanently, and you may decide that other books are important or interesting enough that they will be worth coming back to at a later time. Make sure to save such books so that you do not forget about them. Also, be aware that some books may be above your level, and you can tell that they have vast knowledge stored inside, or great insights, but you are simply not ready for them yet. Put these books aside and return to them when you are ready.

Focus on Understanding, Not Just Facts

Understanding is key. Without understanding, you are unlikely to properly grasp the insights that the book you are reading has to offer. Moreover, without understanding you will be unlikely to remember much, or be able to build properly on your knowledge base in a meaningful way.

Whether you are aiming to get an overview of a book or to read it deeply and absorb it fully, understanding is key. Read a chapter and ask yourself: *Did I understand this? What was the key point? Why did the author find it important enough to write this, and why did he present the material in this way?* If you do not understand something immediately, then you need to ask yourself if it is truly worth understanding. If you jump to the conclusion section of a book first, and you understand perfectly what the author is saying and all the surrounding context, it is likely a topic you know much about and you may gain little value from reading the full book. On the other hand, if you read the conclusion and do not fully understand but you are fascinated, then you may wish to read the book from start to finish to learn about the details and context.

Regurgitating facts has little use in today's world unless you understand the context of those facts, when and how to apply them, and the likely consequences of applying them. Someone who knows some facts but does not know how to implement them properly, may actually be dangerous, misapplying the facts and causing more harm than good.

Instead of disconnected facts, concern yourself with key facts that support your understanding of something important, so that you can gain insights. Build those facts and interrelationships into a story in your mind that expresses the importance of specific insights. Then, store these insights and their related stories in mind so that you are ready to share them when the time is right – it may be with a family member, a friend, a neighbor, a colleague, or even a stranger. This is what the insightful reader does.

Figure Out Word Meanings Without Needing to Know What They Mean

Figuring out the meanings of unknown words is a critical skill that is not emphasized enough in today's world. In society, we tend to emphasize concrete and reliable knowledge, which is important, but sometimes it is also important to develop skills that help you to guess something or figure something out. Not everything in the real world is always crystal clear – sometimes you have to take a guess. Also, we are not computers that have facts implanted into us, sometimes we need to figure them out based on the information we have available. You may be surprised to find that this type of skill is useful not just in reading, but in everyday conversations as well.

The number one way to expand your skill for perceiving the meanings of unknown words is to practice guessing the meanings of words that you do not know. If you are not confident that you guessed right, or you cannot figure it out, then look up the word to see how right or wrong you were. Then, ask yourself if there was enough information in the text where you should have been able to guess the meaning of the word. Make sure to read sentences before and after the mystery word, or even paragraphs before and after it, to make sure you did not miss any key contextual information.

Of course, the richer your vocabulary is to begin with, the more likely you are to figure out a new word. When you understand everything perfectly except for one word on a page, you are much more likely to figure it out, rather than if you are struggling to define a word in each sentence.

One way to help you make sense of words without knowing the meaning would be to study Greek and Latin word roots. If you wish to learn about common word roots and build your vocabulary, you may find *Merriam Webster's Vocabulary Builder* to be beneficial. If you feel that your vocabulary needs to improve, or if English is your second language, you may find this especially worthwhile.

I remember once puzzling over the meaning of a new term in an essay I was reading when I was in high school. I reread the sentence over and over, trying to figure it out. It was a strange term, and so I showed the essay to my father and I asked him for help. He read the passage, appearing to be uncertain at first. He paused for a moment, reading carefully, and then he explained to me exactly what it meant. How did he figure it out? He simply read the sentence after the term, which explained its meaning. This is a silly example, but the lesson to understand here is that many authors will at least attempt to explain unusual words and terms, especially if the reader is not expected to be an expert in the topic.

The point here is to not get so focused on a single word that you lose the context. Look at the surrounding sentences and even paragraphs if you must, to help figure out what a word means. While I have noticed that most people get hung up on the fact that they just read an unusual word or term, I am always considering the full context of a paragraph or a page, rather than focusing too much on a single unknown word. If you know the context, then you know the overall meaning, and all you need to do is fill in what one specific word will likely mean.

If you struggle to determine the meaning of an unknown word, ask yourself a few basic questions: *Is this positive or negative? Big or small? Something abstract or concrete? Is it expressing an emotion or an action? Is it the name of something like a person, building, or city?*

Consider the following examples as a quick exercise on how we can uncover the meanings of words we may not be familiar with.

Example 1: She was fun and *gregarious*, not boring and *insipid.*

Even if you know the meanings of these words, let's pretend that you do not for a moment. You should be able to guess that gregarious is good and related to fun, and insipid is perhaps bad and related to boring in some way. The word "and" is the clue that these are similar or related words. Of course, you may not be able to guess the exact meanings of these words, but you can get an approximate meaning by reading carefully. Other words to pay special attention to are words like "however," "if," "not," or "because." Think of the language logically to guess what a new word could mean, or what it must mean.

Example 2: The boy was highly active. Sometimes he was so adventurous, in fact, that it would backfire on him. Just the other day he ran into the woods completely carefree, and he came back with *splotches* of red all over his legs. It was poison ivy.

Perhaps you do not know what *splotches* means exactly, but if you have ever seen a rash or allergic reaction, you can guess that the word means marks or spots of some kind. If you do not know the precise meaning of the words used above – *gregarious, insipid, splotches* – take a moment to look them up now.

Knowing the meanings of words without having to look them up is a valuable skill to develop, but you should also be prepared to look up new words regularly. The point here is that you should try to figure out the meanings of words *before* looking them up, to strengthen your ability to comprehend unknown words. In time, you may find that you need to look up words less and less, as your vocabulary expands, and you develop a better ability to decipher the meanings of unfamiliar words.

Use Wikipedia, Dictionaries, Google Images, or Other Reference Materials

When you come across something you do not know in a book, and you want to make sure that you are not missing something important, go ahead and look it up. Wikipedia will be a good source of general information and helpful for gaining a background on a topic. For example, if you are reading a book from a soldier's perspective during World War 2, but the book does not actually cover much of the historical context, it could be worth checking out the Wikipedia page on the war to gain a summary level of knowledge and context so that it will be much easier for you to understand this book.

Dictionaries will be worth referring to if you find a word you do not know, or also if you find a word that you think you know, but which is used in an unusual way. Some words can have 20 definitions or more. Therefore, do not assume that just because you have seen a word many times, that you truly know what it means. Also, some words are commonly misused, and you may feel that you know the meaning but be wrong. If you are unsure, look up the word. You should aim to learn several new words or terms from every book you read.

Google Images or other image searching sites will also come in handy when the book discusses a specific bird, tree, musical instrument, or some unusual object is named. Some books can have detailed descriptions of rooftop styles, construction materials, floor tiles, types of hats, or moustaches, and I often think if the writer cared to use technical words and terms, then I should do my part as a reader and develop an accurate mental image of what he is referring to. An image site can do this for you quickly. Even if the author provides a detailed description, an image is often quite powerful in its effect on our understanding.

Signals the Book Gives You to Pay Special Attention

For each heading in a book, make sure you understand the general idea of what the author wants to convey in the section. The heading tells you the key topic that will be discussed, and as mentioned prior, if the topic holds no interest or application for you, you may skip it.

For anything **bolded** or *italicized*, generally make sure that you grasp what these concepts are about. Often these are technical terms, phrases, or ideas. And these will likely be discussed more deeply, meaning it is important that you understand them.

Be sure to pay attention to **technical terms or abbreviations** of such terms, even if they are not bolded or highlighted. If the author mentions the United Nations (UN), then he may discuss it as the UN after that, and you will need to recall what this stands for and what it means. Be aware that authors may define a term once and then never explain it again, assuming that you will recall it. If you are reading a book with much technical terminology, you may take notes on what these terms mean as you read to help make sure that you do not forget the meaning when you see the term mentioned again later.

When the author says things such as **"first," "second," "third,"** and so on, this conveys a list, or an order of importance or perhaps simply the sequence of events, but generally it is helpful to pay attention to the ordering.

With **bullet points**, these will help to digest larger chunks of information and give you the most important or summary points. This will allow you to gain a broader understanding without getting sucked into the details.

Also, pay attention to words that show you **relationships between ideas**. These can be words such as "however," "whereas," "unless," "because," "even though," "despite," and so forth. These types of words present you with a bridge that can help you connect ideas that the author just discussed with ideas that she is about to discuss. Often, these types of words can help you to predict the direction that the author is going to take you.

Lastly, many authors will use **repetition of important themes** to make sure that you understand their full importance. When you see an idea expressed multiple times in a book, you can rest assured that the author thinks this is important for you to learn and to consider deeply.

Good authors often use many of the above tools to capture your attention and alert you, but they do not always do so. Thus, it will be important that you learn to identify the topic that is being discussed, the key terms being used, that you follow the logic of an author from one point to the next, and that you understand on a bullet point (or overview) level what is being said. Ultimately, if the author is not using signals to convey the important points using the above tools, then you may wish to take notes to better organize what you are learning. This is not always necessary, but if you are reading difficult or dense texts, you will find it useful to do so.

Note-Taking – A Comprehensive and Adaptive System

I highly recommend taking notes of some kind, at least for the most valuable books that you read. Although it does take some time, one of the reasons this is so worthwhile is not always the notes themselves, rather it is that taking notes forces you to think more deeply about what you are reading and its importance to you. This is something that many readers do not do, and so they fail to get much value out of their readings. I fought against taking notes for so many years, but some books have been valuable enough to me that I realized I wanted to make sure I would remember them and take action based on them – and notes help greatly with this. If you find it overwhelming thinking that you should go back and take notes on all the books that you have read, do not worry. I would suggest keeping this simple. Occasionally read new books that you think will be highly valuable and take notes on those as you read. Also, occasionally reread books that you found highly useful. When you reread those books, take detailed notes on them as well. Some people may prefer to read a book once without taking any notes, and if the book proves to be worthy, then to go back, reread it, and take notes on it at that time.

Although taking notes can be tedious, this habit is quite useful. This is because instead of feeling the need to reread valuable books every few years, you will be able to simply review your notes, which saves time. You should be aware that there is no shortcut to the notetaking system, such as using someone else's notes instead of actually reading a book. My notes will be especially valuable to me because they are personalized to me, but perhaps your notes will be completely different even for the same book, and yours may hold a lot of value for you but not to me. We all develop a personal relationship with the books we read, and we all absorb unique insights from what we read. Thus, you must take your own notes to gain the full benefits from them.

The following are the most important elements to keep in mind as you take notes on your readings.

Do not take verbatim notes

Taking notes verbatim is quite tempting and I have already tried it in the past, so I feel that it needs mentioning. *Do not* take verbatim notes – many e-readers make it easy to highlight and then export your highlights, but this is not as useful as it may sound. When you write down or copy and paste notes word for word, your mind does little thinking. Then when you read over your notes later, your mind is not properly active, because the words were not truly your own. In order to recall information, you must make it your own. You must morph and adapt the information to your specific needs, or it will simply not stick. This is a mistake I have made in the past, and I would urge you to avoid it.

Another key issue with taking verbatim notes is that you will tend to take far too many notes, much more than is truly necessary. You can always copy down some quotes, but if you are quoting large sections of the book, this will not be so useful.

You must make the book your own through your note-taking and transform it into something other than what the original author may have even intended. We are all in our own unique mind frames, circumstances, with our own histories, and our own spin or adaptation on everything that we are exposed to. Even identical twins are different based on their individual experiences. Whatever you learn from a book will be different than what anyone else would have learned from the same book. Let this be reflected in the unique notes that you take.

Goal

As discussed earlier: What is your goal (or goals) for reading the book you chose? What do you hope to learn? Ideally, you should record this *before* you read a book. If at any point you realize that the book will not teach you what you are looking for, you may abandon it. My general goal is to gain insights, but if I have a specific goal for a book, I always aim to keep it in mind. Write down your goal, or you may confuse your personal goal with the goal that the author provides within the book. The two goals do not always coincide.

Quotes

Quotes can be powerful because they often carry a great deal of information in a short space. They can be wonderful to share with others too. A short and powerful quote may be impactful enough to you that you use it to guide your life decisions, or you may post it in front of your desk as a reminder of what truly matters. Some of the best quotes I have read will stick in my mind and I will think about them over and over, considering their deep importance. If you like quotes, you may be interested in a book I published that collects powerful and inspirational quotes. The eBook is available for free, and the title is ***365 Quotes to Live Your Life By***. I hope you take a minute of your time to download it online (e.g., on Amazon or other retailers).

As you read a book, if there are any quotes that stick out to you and that you would like to reflect on more deeply, then I recommend writing these down. It is often preferable to take notes in your own words, but if you especially like the way a sentence or a few sentences were worded, you may wish to preserve the exact message. Generally, I write down 1-5 key quotes from the books that I read. I will caution you once more against storing too many notes verbatim. Observe your tendencies and if you tend to take excessive notes in this way, you should reconsider your process.

Insights

As you know, my primary reason for reading is to gain insights, and so I always make sure to write down notes on any insights that I gain. Most books will not have more than one insight, but some may have several. These will be important lessons that you want to make sure never to forget.

When you have an insight, I would urge you to immediately write this down, either in a notebook where you take notes on books you read, or in a separate notebook specifically for insights if you prefer. You do not want to risk forgetting these later.

When deciding whether something is an insight, ask yourself:

- Is this a point that could change my life?
- Does this completely change the way I think about something?
- Does this reveal something new to me that I had never thought about, that will have great implications?
- Is this something I think everyone should know, but I feel that most people are not aware of?

Key Points

Key points are usually facts that support insights, or they are interesting points worth reflecting on, but do not necessarily provide you with an insight. These are points that you may want to discuss with others or apply in your life in some way. Some of your key points may be key terms that you want to define for yourself, which describe something important you want to make sure to recall. Usually I will write down somewhere from 5-20 key points, depending on how useful the book was to me.

Summary & Reflections

If you often find that after a few years of reading a book you forget what it was about, you may benefit from noting down a summary of what you read. Also, it is natural to record your general thoughts and why this book was particularly important for you or what it meant to you in your life. This format can become a sort of journal of your life through books. Later on, you can go back and see the growth, development, and maturation of your thoughts and actions, as you read more books. If you like writing book reviews, you may use these thoughts or at least some parts of them to write a review on sites such as Amazon or Goodreads. You would be surprised at just how much writers appreciate receiving thoughtful reviews. I do not always take notes on my *Summary & Reflections*, but if I do, generally a paragraph or two is good enough. Of course, if you are deeply impacted by a book, you may be inclined to write more.

Questions

It can be helpful to keep track of any questions that arise as you read. If you wait until the end of your readings, you may forget what your questions were. As you read, pay attention to any questions that begin to form in your mind. Do not dismiss them – write them down. When you finish the book, you may answer all of your own questions that you can, given what you learned from reading. If any questions remain unanswered and they are important to you, you can pursue other books that will help you to answer them.

I cannot emphasize the following enough. **What holds most people back from being star readers is that they do not question.** This means they are reading passively, just taking information in. Instead, you need to treat reading as a mental sport. You take in information through reading, but you should also be producing questions based on that information, and this will drive your curiosity to learn and read more. You must demand to learn something from what you read, and not take it in as if you were a prisoner to the book. Be an active participant. This is a show where the magician invites you to the stage, not one where you stay in your seat to passively observe the whole time. Through experiencing the magic for yourself, you will be transformed.

If you do not have questions at first, do not worry. Make it your goal to ask one new question from every book you read. In time, you will find that you form more and more questions, and an endless curiosity will arise out of you from this one simple habit.

Bright Ideas

Bright ideas are similar to insights, but they are not quite the same. Instead, bright ideas are your own unique ideas that arose from something you read. Perhaps you thought of how to apply something from a book in a new and creative way, and you would like to invent something or start a business based on what you read. This is not an insight that the author provided, but rather one that you formed yourself based on ideas from the book. Insights and bright ideas are basically the same thing, but insights are provided by the author, and bright ideas are provided by yourself, using the author's ideas as inspiration.

Action

What is one action you plan to take based on what you have read? This is critical, as this is where you convert thoughts and ideas into reality, making an impact on the world. An action may be that you will apply a new principle, that you will donate to a charity, or that you will discuss something in the book with someone you know who is knowledgeable in the topic. Alternatively, you may advise or help someone with a problem, based on what you learned. Anything at all that you plan to do in the real world as a result of your reading is an action.

The student becomes the master not just by reading, but by doing. To become a master at something, or at many things, you will need to read, take action based on what you read, see the results, and adjust your reading habits and actions based on those results.

Further Reading

As you read a book, sometimes an author will mention a book that she read and liked, or a book that made some important points, and you may be intrigued by the title or concept. Write down such book titles or add then to your "to reads" list. You can always choose to read it later or not – but the point is that you should make note of the title so as not to forget it. Also, there may be a list of further books to read in a "reference" or "further readings" section of the book. If some of these book titles capture your attention, be sure to write them down as well. Aim to discover one new book to read, from every book you read.

Do not overwhelm yourself

If you are getting started with taking notes, start with one or two of the elements described above. After you take notes on several books this way, perhaps start taking notes on more of the elements. Do not force yourself to take notes on ALL of the above points. Just take notes on the ones that are more natural or the ones that you feel will be most useful to you, depending on the book, and depending on your objectives for the book.

How I take notes

I keep in mind all of the above points, but I do not worry about them as I read. Instead, I make sure to focus my mind on what I read, and that I understand and gain the most use from what I am reading. Generally, I will have a specific notebook for taking notes about books. I highly recommend this, to keep it separate from any other notes you may take for work or for your personal life. If you prefer, take notes on your computer – such as on Google Docs or Evernote – which are free applications to use.

When I read, I will have my notebook open, and I will take different types of notes for different types of books. If a book has many interesting and challenging ideas, I may summarize the book as I go, to make sure I am fully understanding what the author says. When I read books with many unfamiliar key terms, I spend time writing down what these terms mean in my own words. In the case where a book makes me wonder and sparks many questions, I will document my questions and reflect on their implications. For a fictional book, I may write down what I think the larger purpose or message is that the author is trying to convey. Either way, for every chapter or section, I like to take at least a few notes to demonstrate what I got out of it. To have no notes is like telling myself that reading the chapter was not even worth it. If I read a few chapters without feeling the need to take any notes, then this is a signal that the book is not useful or that I am not properly understanding what I read.

For me, it is important to write my notes down as I read, because if I wait until I finish the book, I find that too often my mind was in passive mode, and I struggle to think of what I truly gained from the book. Also, I may struggle to remember my thoughts and what I found to be important after finishing the book. I do not have a bad memory, but there are many levels of tasks happening in book reading: understanding what the author says, what he truly means, what the implications of his statements are, judging whether his assumptions and logic are sound and whether his biases interfere with the accuracy of his statements, gathering the book's key insights, asking questions that are not yet resolved in the book, and figuring out what information from the book is actionable. If these processes are not being executed while reading, it becomes difficult to backtrack and initiate them *after* finishing a book. After I have my handwritten notes from the book, I will think through them more carefully and polish them up, type them out, and save them on my computer. From then on, I should not need to reread the book, as I have my notes organized and saved. Of course, for the best books that you read, you may wish to reread them occasionally even if you took good notes.

On the other hand, sometimes I simply highlight (if an eBook) or draw a bracket on the side of the page (if a paper book) for certain parts. I aim to do this minimally, to make sure I focus on important or potentially insightful information. Keep in mind that highlighting too many parts of the book defeats the purpose. Then when I finish reading, I reexamine these parts and take notes on them, after having the benefit of having read the full book. If you wish to keep reading and notetaking separate, then you may prefer this style of notetaking.

My notetaking system is adaptive, which means you can adapt it to your particular needs. For some especially valuable reads, you may take more notes and in greater depth, and for shorter books or reads that are not as valuable, you may take less notes. You can take notes in different ways for different types of books.

Review your notes

I recommend reviewing some of your notes at least periodically. Reviewing your notes will help you to internalize and apply them in your life. Ultimately, reviewing your notes will help you to see if you are making progress based on what you have read. If you read a book that you thought made a huge impact on you, but you check your notes and find that you have not applied any of the principles and nothing in your life has changed for the better, then this is a hint that you need to get into the habit of applying what you read.

Reviewing your notes will be critical for remembering what you read years after having read a book. After many years, you will not necessarily need to recall the book verbatim, but you should at least recall what made the book important to you and what insights you gained from it.

If in time you find that some books you thought were important ended up not being relevant or useful for you anymore, you can always delete such books from your notes. I do not like to delete anything, so I would probably move such notes into an archives file so that I know it is no longer important to me – but it would still be there just in case. You can choose what works best for you.

You can see *Example Notes for The Insightful Reader* (at the end of this book) if you would like to see an example of how someone may take notes on the book you are reading now.

Tips for Reading Different Book Types

The following tips are meant to make it easier for you to read more broadly and in areas that perhaps did not interest you much in the past, or in areas that you were intimidated to begin reading in. Keep in mind that the best way to learn to read in a genre and become good at it is to read more of it.

For all genres

I advise reading from different types of authors – male and female, and from different countries and ethnicities. Often, you are more likely to gain new and profound insights from other cultures and peoples' who you are less familiar with. When you read only books by authors from your country, your gender, your political beliefs, religious beliefs, and so on, everything tends to make sense and is easy. The true challenge comes when you read books by an author who has a completely different life than you. Then you are stretched to entertain ideas that you never even thought a person might reasonably entertain. Keep an open mind to new ideas and perspectives, and understand that your own beliefs and perspectives may seem quite strange to someone who has not had any prior exposure to them.

History

Why are things happening as they do? With history, it is easy to get lost in the details. Wars are fought for years and the actual reasons tend to be forgotten or misunderstood. Remember to read with the aim of understanding *why* things happened as they did. You can read about *what* happened quite easily, but you will likely be forced to think more carefully if you wish to fully comprehend why events transpired as they did.

With history books, make sure that you keep in mind the general dates involved such as the decade or century, but do not worry too much about remembering every date. Of course, for highly important dates such as the start and end of the world wars, or for any other major events that pique your interest, you may wish to remember those dates. However, in general, while dates are important to establish context and order, they do not need to be memorized.

You will want to consider the general context of the historic period. If it is not well explained in one book, you may seek out other books or sources that elaborate on what the daily living circumstances were like for civilians, for soldiers, and for the rich or the poor. Ask yourself questions such as: Who was the leader in charge and what type of government was in place? Did people generally feel free or were they ruled over ruthlessly? What were the main concerns people had?

If you are bad with remembering names, you may keep your own list of notes on important people. You can note what they were best known for, their formal titles or statuses, and a description of their personalities and goals.

When reading history, do not assume that one historian or author has offered you the full picture of what happened. Rather, read different accounts of the same historic events, as often there are deeply conflicting stories, depending on which side is telling the story, or depending on what bias the historian or writer has.

To get started with reading in history, I recommend *A History of the World in 6 Glasses* by Tom Standage, *Big History* by Cynthia Stokes Brown, and *Guns, Germs, & Steel* by Jared Diamond.

Science

Pay special attention to foundational rules and themes. For example, foundational rules may be Newton's three laws of motion, or the four laws of thermodynamics. It will be key that you understand such key equations or principles in physics before moving on to more complex ideas.

When reading about science and math, it is critical that you understand one idea before moving on to the next. If you did not fully grasp an important idea, you will often fail to grasp the next key idea and the next. This may require a great amount of patience from you, as you will need to read slowly, reread, or seek outside materials to aid in your understanding at times.

I would advise that if you are not an expert in science, that you pick up multiple foundational texts, perhaps covering different themes. It would be wise to pick up books that cover general scientific ideas to provide you with an overview – in biology, chemistry, physics, and other natural phenomena, for example. If you feel particularly weak in science, you may pick up several basic science books to help make sure that you grasp these concepts fully before advancing.

To get started with science, I would recommend *A Short History of Nearly Everything by* Bill Bryson, *Astrophysics for People in a Hurry* by Neil DeGrasse Tyson, and *The Gene* by Siddhartha Mukherjee.

Personal Development

With personal development, the key that many people miss is that they should take action based on what they learn. These books are not theoretical – you are meant to apply what they teach, and then perhaps the greatest lessons will come from the results you get when you apply what you have read.

Think about which areas you want to improve in the most and read books that focus on those specific topics. Is it in your learning, your socializing, your ability to understand yourself, your happiness? What is it? When you figure it out, read books on that topic.

With personal development books, sometimes the author's personality will clash with your own, or a different approach will work for him than what works for you. As you read, you may get a sense that you are on the same page as with some authors, whereas for others the advice given may not seem appropriate. The tricky part is that you should be open-minded to new approaches, but you should also be aware that some authors may give tips that truly do not resonate with your way of being. As an example, some books may advise that lying is appropriate if you judge that it will help you succeed. If you believe in being as ethical as you can be, such advice will not work for you. In this case, it may be best to seek out a different book – or of course you may finish it to understand the lengths other people are willing to go to succeed, without succumbing to it yourself.

To get started in self-development, read *The Four Agreements* by Don Miguel Ruiz, *Choose Yourself* by James Altucher, and *Mastery* by Robert Greene.

Biographies

Reading the life stories of other people can be highly encouraging and valuable, as you can learn profound and inspiring life lessons without going through the trials and tribulations yourself. With these books you can often learn a mixture of history, science, business, self-development, and other areas depending on who is the focus of the biography.

When reading biographies, you should pay attention to general principles that you can apply, yet consider that often the way that the person in the book applied them will not be the same way that you will need to apply them. We all live in a unique social and historical context, and you have to keep that in mind whenever you wish to apply advice that worked for someone from another time and place, with their own social and historical context.

If you are not aware of the key differences from the time and place of the book to your own, hopefully the book you are reading will illuminate some of those for you, or you may wish to do your own research. Some basic ideas to keep in mind are how much the population size has changed, how much inflation has changed the value of money, whether it was a time of war, and who the president was or what type of government was in place. Also, what was the socioeconomic status of the subject?

Two of my favorite biographies are survival oriented – *Into the Wild* by Jon Krakauer and *438 Days* by Jonathan Franklin. Some other excellent biographies to check out are: *Gifted Hands* by Ben Carson, *The Autobiography of Malcolm X* by Malcolm X and Alex Haley, and *Leonardo da Vinci* by Walter Isaacson.

Philosophy

When reading philosophy, keep in mind the basic assumptions that the author makes, and ask whether you agree with them, or what basis there is to believe in these assumptions. You may find some of those assumptions to be wrong, unprovable or unable to be disproven, or debatable at least. If so, consider how valuable the rest of the book will actually be. Of course, even if a book has invalid assumptions, if it is a philosophy book, you may gain something by following along with how a respected philosopher thought about things. You may also learn something by searching for their mistakes and analyzing the problems in their thought processes that led to those mistakes.

Consider whether the area of philosophy you are interested in has been figured out by science. In some cases, as the field of science began through philosophical inquiry, science may have figured out some of the questions that were discussed in older philosophy books. Through history, concepts such as the atom were philosophical ideas that could not be observed or experimented upon. Of course, through modern science we have observed and experimented with atoms. Their existence is no longer a matter of debate, perspective, or philosophy. To learn about such topics, you will benefit more from reading in science than in philosophy.

Something to be aware of is that philosophy has largely been a record of human thought on a variety of issues – love, the meaning of life, the nature of reality, human perception, God and religion, ethics, logic, how to live a good life, and so forth. This has not been a linear progression, but rather one that has involved conflicts of opinion and differing perspectives – and many philosophical issues have not been resolved, but rather continue to be debated and are ever-evolving. For the reader of philosophy, there is rarely one correct solution, but rather, you must become aware of the issues, of the perspectives of respected philosophers, and then decide what you believe is the truth.

It is critical to remember *not* to accept what is stated at face value. Think of it deeply on your own and ask if this could truly be the case and decide if you agree with what is being said. Do not read philosophy as a series of facts, read it as a series of propositions or interpretations that you must reinterpret for yourself. The true value in philosophy is not in assuming that the philosophers (even if famous or well-known) know everything, it is in building your own interpretations of what the philosophers knew or thought they knew, and in reevaluating what you think about yourself and the world. As you read philosophy, remember that there is value in struggling through such books even if you disagree with every word – this is because if you had not read the book, you would not have realized just how strongly you disagreed with certain ideas. Ultimately, exposing yourself to ideas that conflict with what you know and believe, even erroneous and malformed ideas, will help you to nurture your mind into becoming more critical and insightful.

You may have noticed this if you ever attempted to read classical philosophical works, but they are generally not light or easy reads. Thus, it can be useful to read summaries of philosophers and their beliefs, either through books or perhaps articles or websites, and then to decide for yourself if there is a particular philosopher or philosophical period that you would like to learn about more deeply.

To start with philosophy, I advise learning more about Stoic philosophy, as this is an applied and practical philosophy to help us all live a better life. A good overview of Stoic philosophy is *A Guide to the Good Life* by William B. Irvine. For an overview of philosophy as a whole, you may read *The Philosophy Book* by Will Buckingham or *The Great Philosophers* by Bryan Magee. For a deeper level summary and analysis, read *The Story of Philosophy* by Will Durant. Other books to read are *Meditations* by Marcus Aurelius and *The Heart of the Buddha's Teaching* by Thich Nhat Hánh.

Literature

Classical works are often a good starting point if you want to read fiction. These books have been studied for decades or more because they have aspired to enlighten us with universal truths about the human condition. They tend to have many complex themes and many different ways to interpret the meaning and significance of the events that transpire. If you open your mind, you can always find a parallel to what is happening inside the novel and what is happening in the real world. This is likely what contributes to these books becoming classics – there are important themes for everyone to think about: life and death, love and loss, desire and dread, the haves and the have-nots, meaning and lack thereof, creation and destruction, the pursuit of money and power, and different ways of thinking, living, and being.

Be prepared to read these books more slowly, as often there is much more happening than what it seems on the surface. You may have to read between the lines to build your own interpretations, rather than just accepting what is stated at face value. The complexities of humanity are likely to shine through, as sometimes we say one thing and mean another, or do something appearing confident while trembling with fear on the inside. A reoccurring theme will be how our thoughts, words, and actions are not always in sync, and the key question will be what the meaning of this is. In the end, an overarching question will arise: *Who are we, really? What defines humanity?*

Most of *The Insightful Reader* applies to reading nonfiction. However, reading fiction will still play an important role in your intellectual and creative development. Now I would like you to consider that reading nonfiction and fiction will require different types of mindsets. With nonfiction, your mindset will typically be goal oriented and functional. You will read a book with a particular aim or objective – then you will pursue insights and the collections of facts that help to support those insights.

With fiction, it is not always clear exactly where a journey will take you. You do not want to do too much research into a book before reading it because this will likely spoil it for you. With fiction, some people do not even wish to read the back cover or the snippets of reviews and laudatory comments that are sometimes in the beginning pages, as these may somehow spoil the experience. Thus, when preparing to read fiction I will do a brief search on Goodreads, to find a useful book in a topic of interest. As another option, I may pursue recommendations from people I trust, or simply read well known classics. You have to be ready for a journey, and you have to be in a patient frame of mind. If you need immediate utility from the words you read, you will be annoyed at reading fiction and your mind will not prosper from the experience.

Note that some people may say that if they were going to read fiction, they would rather watch a movie. But there is a key element missing from the movies that you get with fiction. With fiction, you can get inside the minds of characters. You can know what they are thinking, whereas with movies you often have to guess what the characters are thinking. Getting into characters' minds is of value because this will help you to better understand why people in the real world behave as they do. Through fiction, we can gain a greater understanding of humanity than we sometimes can with nonfiction. Many research studies have also shown that reading fiction helps us to build our empathy for others – I believe this is because you can often explore people's lives more deeply through fiction than with the alternatives.

I would now like to provide you with a tip for reading a specific genre that I find highly valuable. When reading speculative fiction (e.g., fantasy or science fiction), do not question what is happening too much. Allow the world to take you over as if it were a dream world that you entered, and this was an alternate universe that you were absorbed into. The more you question the world and resist it, the more you will be taken out of the experience. While with nonfiction we question and look for flaws, sometimes questioning too much can ruin fiction. The fictional world does not need to be perfectly true, after all it is made up – and there will be some aspects that defy the laws and rules as we know them to be in our world. That is perfectly fine – fiction is meant to expand possibilities, not restrict them – and hopefully to expand our minds in the process.

A word of caution – some fiction or even narrative nonfiction books have an "Introduction" or "Foreword" section where an author or editor will discuss the general themes of the book and give background information. If you are reading a book for the first time, I recommend skipping this part as it will likely contain major spoilers. For example, if a central character dies, this part of the book may reveal why the character needed to die, ruining it for a first-time reader.

Some of my favorite fiction books are *1984* by George Orwell, *The Alchemist* by Paulo Coelho, *Flowers for Algernon* by Daniel Keyes, *One Flew Over the Cuckoo's Nest* by Ken Kesey, *The Executioner's Song* by Norman Mailer (based on a true story), *Stoner* by John Williams, and *Blindness* by José Saramago.

Tips for Reading Very Challenging Material

If you think a book may be too advanced for you, then examine it thoroughly to get an idea of how difficult of a read this may be. The more challenging it is, the more you need to start studying it early and follow the tips I have outlined for you below. If you wait too long to start reading, then you may not have enough time to digest and learn the material, if this is for an assignment or if you have a deadline. A general theme with these tips will be that you have to be willing to take your learning beyond the book. The book can only tell you so much, and sometimes it will be of greater help to seek *outside* materials which can help you better understand what is *inside* the book.

Seek contextual information

You can do this via Wikipedia or other encyclopedias to help you better understand the general framework or context that surrounds the book. If you are learning about DNA but your book assumes a general understanding, you may prefer to read background information through another source first, where you can refresh yourself on basic facts that your advanced text does not cover. For example, through outside sources, you may review that DNA makes up genes, genes make up chromosomes, and chromosomes are inside the nucleus of a cell. This type of review can help you to make sure that you have learned the fundamentals of a topic. Then, this will help you to stay focused when you are reading advanced texts which assume you already have such a general understanding. When seeking to understand the context, you can ask: *How does the concept I wish to learn about fit into other concepts I am already aware of?* Or you may ask: *Where, when, how, and why does this concept take place?*

Learn about the author

Who is your author? Learning more about him can often help you to more deeply understand the subject matter. Did he go to war, was he a professor, has he been in trouble with the law? Is he a political activist? What country or city does he live in? Is he a theoretician or a practitioner? Such information may provide unexpected clues to help you understand the text. Often, at the end of a book there is more information about the author. If not, usually you can find it online on the site where you purchase books, or on his personal website. Also, keep in mind that some authors allow you to contact them via email (e.g., mine is ic.robledo@mentalmax.net) or via a contact page on their website. If you have any specific questions, you may be able to ask directly.

Read reviews

Read reviews from critics and general readers – to gain a better idea of what types of insights you were supposed to have gathered from the reading material. Sometimes a reviewer will provide important contextual information or break down complex ideas into something simpler that will be easier for you to follow. There may even be some reviewers who express that the book was very difficult to read, and that they benefited from reading other books first. After reading such reviews and recommended readings, you will likely be more prepared to read the book you initially wanted to read.

Read more basic books first

Often you can read a basic book rather quickly, and then you will feel more prepared to read the book you actually want to focus on. If you read a few basic books and still feel lost, be aware that you may need to invest more time in learning the fundamentals before you will be ready to tackle more advanced material. These fundamental books will elaborate ideas much more thoroughly instead of assuming that you already understand them, which will help you to make much more progress in your learning. **When aiming to learn something challenging, taking a step back and slowing down is more effective than rushing and attempting to leap forward.**

Meet with other people who are reading the same book to discuss it

If you are in a class it may be convenient to discuss the book with fellow classmates, or you may find a forum online where people discuss what they think the book means, or why it was important for them. For challenging books, it can be useful to discuss them with others who may also be struggling to understand. Often, you will find that parts which did not make sense to you did make sense for others, and vice versa – allowing you to help each other make progress in your understanding. You can also seek out communities online (e.g., Facebook groups, Reddit, or other forums) if you are not aware of anyone else who is reading the same book.

Take notes as you go, rather than waiting to finish the book

For extremely dense and difficult books, such as a textbook or other highly advanced or technical texts, rather than taking notes on the book as a whole after you finish, you may take notes on sections. For example, what were the impressionable quotes, insights, key points, your summary & reflections, questions, etc., for the first chapter or section of the book, then move on the next section and ask yourself these questions once again, and so forth. You want to be sure that you fully understand one section of a difficult book before proceeding to the next. It is of no value to plow through a difficult book, to reach the end, and claim that you read it and yet understanding nothing. Take it chapter by chapter. If there is just one section that is very difficult to comprehend, you may skip it and come back to it later. But if you find that every section presents great challenges, do not continue to read assuming it will all make sense later. Be prepared to slow down and to back up if necessary.

Write down all of your questions and seek answers from the book you are reading

If you cannot find the answers to your questions in your book, then seek them online. If you still cannot find them, seek out experts who may be able to help you. To advance in your understanding, you should seek the answers to your own questions. A book is a tool and a guide, but ultimately you must have your own ideas, interests, and questions that guide you along in your readings.

Seek out supplementary learning materials

Some challenging books come with a CD or supplementary materials of some kind. Perhaps there is software or a learning tool that is accessible via a website that the book recommends. Even if the book does not include such materials, you may seek out your own resources to supplement what you are learning. For example, a book on language learning could be too limited in its usefulness, and you may seek out videos for free online, or software that shows you how native speakers pronounce words in another language. Often, different types of media will help us to see how something applies in the real world. As another example, if you read a book about volunteer work, you may discover many ways that you can volunteer in your community. But it can also be helpful to see what it looks like when communities work together for a common good. Through pictures, video, or interactive media, you can build a more accurate picture of how concepts apply in the real world, which will help to supplement what you have learned through books. Of course, there are other ways to supplement your learning – you may interview an expert, go to a museum, or visit a new place, for example.

Get a tutor or seek in depth learning assistance

If the material is highly difficult and you are not making much progress on your own, you may seek help from someone who can help explain it to you, such as an expert. When you are struggling deeply with learning something, often this is an option worth considering, as tutors will be able to explain difficult material in a way that is more understandable. Some topics are deeply complex and finding a real person who can help to identify your weak spots and strengthen them could be the most valuable path. If you know that a particular topic is always a challenge for you, this can be a useful route to take – finding a tutor before you get too frustrated. Of course, not all tutors are equal – you should take the time to pursue one who works well for your needs.

Read *more* books that are very challenging

Doing this will help you to develop your reading skills and to improve. Seek out those books which introduce ideas you have never even considered and those that use new words that you had not seen before. Pursue those books that make you think in new ways. Read in topics that arouse wonder and awe from you, and read through them carefully and thoroughly, to make sure that you understand. In today's society we are obsessed with speed, but often reading speedily is only an option on very simple, easy, direct texts. But the books with truly deep and profound ideas should not be read so quickly. You need time to reflect and read between the lines of the text. You should aspire to produce questions and think, rather than zooming through everything without reflection or true understanding. Do not be afraid of attempting to read books which present you with challenges. Actually, seek them out. These are the ones which will ultimately provide you with the most insights and help to improve your critical thinking and reading abilities.

What to Do When You Are Lost and Confused

It happens to everyone – you reach a point in your readings where you realize that you were reading passively, almost falling asleep, or passing your eyes over the words without truly processing what you were reading. Now you are confused, unable to understand what the author means at the point you have reached, and you have a decision to make. Do you continue reading despite having clearly missed something, or do you go back?

Your choice depends on your goals and on the type of book. Is this book very challenging, with large amounts of information tightly packed, where you could easily miss something important if you lost focus? Then go back and continue at the point where you originally had a lapse in attention. You may even reread the whole section if you want to make sure you understood everything.

On the other hand, if it is an easy read, with sections that have a main point, elaborations on those points, and then summary sections, it may not be important to go back and see where you got lost. You should be quite likely to figure it out, or possibly not even have missed anything important.

A way to help prevent getting lost and confused is to read in shorter intervals. If this happens to you often, read with a specific purpose, and read sitting down in a chair with your back straight instead of leaning back or lying down. Also, avoid reading while tired. Generally, be comfortable but do not get too comfortable so that you can focus on your reading.

If the above advice does not help you improve much, you have to ask what is happening. Is the material simply too difficult or complex for you? If so, then perhaps you should find a more suitable book for your level. An alternative is that the book may not be as appealing as you originally expected. Then, you may need to find a book with similar content that presents the material in a more interesting way.

Author Motive and Bias

Ask why the author wrote a book to begin with. You have your purposes in reading a book, but do not forget that the author has his own purpose in writing it. Is his purpose first and foremost to help you to learn something? Does it seem that he rambles and is writing more to make himself feel better or to brag about his own accomplishments, rather than to simply help the reader? Does the author have an agenda so strong that he is not seeing truth as it is, but rather he is in the business of creating his own truth and convincing others of it? For example, some people in politics appear to work in this way, where they aim to convince people of the particular story that they want to tell which benefits themselves and their own party. The facts do not seem to matter as much as their will to tell a story that makes themselves look good and others look bad.

Asking why the author wrote the book may help you to figure out whether you can truly trust what has been said inside of it. The authors I prefer to read from are those who prioritize the truth above all else. This is harder than you would think, for any time we tell a story, we risk having our personal biases get in the way of truth. Another risk is that we tend to avoid hurting other people's feelings. We also do not want to make ourselves look bad. But the reality is that humans have done things which are of course not noble or glorious or beneficial in any way, at times. In certain cases, we have done the most atrocious things, and books can help us to learn about why this happens. If the author is too concerned with making sure that everyone is happy with what the book says and that no one's feelings are hurt, then we will not be able to get at the real truth of the matter. Niceties can be useful for interacting with people on a personal level, but when reading to understand the reality, they get in the way of building knowledge and understanding for ourselves.

It helps to know the author's background and experiences, to be able to better judge what he says. Did he grow up in the Americas, Europe, or Asia? Was he raised rich or poor? Is he well educated, self-taught, or not especially knowledgeable? Has he been independent most of his life, or dependent on others? What religion is he, and what political party? These things matter because they tend to bias us. Someone who grew up in a traditional and stable household may think strongly that this is the standard we should all be judged on, and someone who did not grow up this way may think that there are many kinds of households one could grow up in and still become a good citizen of the world. However, do not assume that an author is heavily biased simply because of his background. The best authors will be able to understand their own biases and pursue the truth regardless of it. I do not recommend looking deeply into every author you read, but if you find an author to be deeply influential, it could be worth learning about his or her background. This may help you to better interpret the meaning of his books.

After Reading

An Introduction

There is still work to be done even after you have finished a book. If you have done your work of being a good reader though, this part should go rather smoothly. By now, you should have already thought through *why* you were reading your book and *what* you wanted to learn from it. If you heeded my suggestions, you have also taken notes on what you read, so now you can simply focus on *reviewing what you learned* and *taking action* based on this. In this section we will discuss how to get the most from what you already read.

Discuss the Book

I find that it is always a big help to discuss something that I have read. You may discuss the themes of a book with people that you know – perhaps a spouse, family member, friend, or colleague. When you summarize or explain what you read, often the person you discuss it with will lack context, and so they may ask some questions. Those questions will function as a useful quiz to help make sure that you learned something and that you truly understood the book you just read. They may also help to spark your curiosity if they ask interesting questions you had not considered, and you may become curious enough to want to read more books on the topic.

For the books that leave a deep impact on you, you will probably find that you truly want to discuss them, because you will think that these are ideas which could benefit many individuals. Be open to engaging in such conversations with a wide range of people. There is no need to feel that you can only discuss a book with people who have already read it. You can always introduce the topic of a book, or the main idea. Most people will be able to understand if you take a moment to explain – you may be surprised to find that some people will have interesting perspectives on a topic, even if they have not necessarily read the same book.

If you enjoy the idea of discussing what you read, you may be interested in seeking out book clubs as well. Although I am not a member of any book clubs and do not have experience with this, you may find some value in it. You could even consider starting your own club. Alternatively, you can search for book reader groups or forums online where you can discuss a book. Or if you prefer, you can simply journal your own thoughts about a book and reflect on them.

Create an Action Plan

Create an action plan (i.e., a plan to take specific actions) based on the book you just read. Even if all you plan to do is implement one action, you should form a plan and schedule it in your calendar for when you plan to do it. Loose plans in our mind or thinking "I really should do X" is not good enough. Those types of "plans" are rarely completed.

An issue with having loose plans is that it is easy to read a book, put it aside, and think *I know what to do, so I will go ahead and implement the tips the author mentioned later.* Then in time other things come up, we may read other books, and we probably forget many of the tips from the original book. In time, we are likely to forget about the issues we wanted to fix in the first place, or we simply keep applying our same old systems that are suboptimal, due to habit. Instead, the best thing to do is to form plans right after reading a book for what we *will* do. You should aim to write down actions that are concrete and time-based. If you read a book about improving friendships, for example, you may decide that you should do something nice for a friend, but of course this is not a concrete plan. Instead, you could make an action plan to give an especially helpful friend a gift to show your appreciation, making a note of the date by which you plan to do this. Of course, the actions that you plan should be ones that you would not have planned to do without the aid of the book you read.

If you struggle to implement action plans due to limited time, or because your interests shift rapidly, you may simply write down one action you would like to complete for a given book. Do not overcomplicate this. A simple action could be thinking of the person who needs this information most, then calling and informing her about what you learned.

Take Notes or Update the Ones You Already Took

From every book you read: aim to *at least* **have one goal**, **ask one question**, **gain one insight**, **take one action**, **discover a new book to read,** and **write down a way to improve your reading process** (we will discuss this more soon). You can get these from truly valuable books. If you are not coming away with such concepts from the books you read, then you should be more careful about what you choose to read and try to improve your process. If you find all the note-taking tips described earlier to be overwhelming, I recommend taking notes just on what has been bolded above. Then if you have additional notes, you can simply write down your "additional notes" in freestyle, without worrying about categorizing them. Perhaps you have additional questions, thoughts, or you realize the great implications of one of the insights you learned. If so, these will be excellent points to take further notes on.

Important Lists to Maintain

Do not forget to maintain your "to reads" and "books read" lists, and a separate list for the best or "most insightful books" you have read. You will want to keep track of your books, to make sure that you focus more on the ones that are most useful for your needs, or which you have enjoyed the most. Recall that it is easy to maintain these lists with an app such as Goodreads. If you wish, you may review an earlier section where this was discussed in more depth.

Evaluate Your Reading Process

After you have finished a book, consider how useful it was. Did you learn what you were expecting to? If you did not, did you start reading with a purpose in mind? Was there a problem with your reading process, or was it simply not the right book for you at this time? If there was an issue with the quality of the book, should you have noticed this before beginning it? For example, when you picked up the book did you check the cover, title, and description thoroughly? Did you read some passages from the book first before choosing to purchase or download it? Did you evaluate the book as you read, and abandon it if you realized it was not a valuable read, or did you keep reading from start to finish without analyzing its contents? The bottom line here is you should critique your own reading process to see if there is something you could have done better. To improve as a reader, you have to think about your reading skills and habits and aim to improve them.

Remember that it is not a failure on your part to abandon a book. Not all books are right for you or useful for your specific purposes. The more quickly you abandon the wrong books, the more time you can spend reading the valuable ones that you will enjoy and benefit from. If you never abandon any books, you are probably not spending your time reading the best books for you and this is something you should focus on changing.

After you finish reading a book, aim to write down one thing you could have done better in your reading process. Would putting the author's name in a search engine have helped you to determine that he was not qualified to write on the topic he chose? Did you read through the whole book without taking any notes, then get to the end without having gained much from the experience? Was it a bad idea to accept a book recommendation from someone you barely knew? Did you waste time reading parts that had no relevance or value for you? Did you read through dense and difficult parts too quickly and fail to understand them? What is something you could have done better? Write this down so that you do not make the same mistake next time you read a book.

What to Read Next?

Read the same book again

If you feel that you read the book too fast or you skipped through many sections, or it was highly valuable and you are worried that you did not understand everything, then you may elect to read the same book again, or at least to put it on a list where you will plan to read it again later.

Read other books from the same author

If the book was very insightful or useful to you, consider reading more books from the same author. Often, if the author wrote one book that you truly enjoyed, he will also have written other books that you would benefit from as well, and they are much more likely to be in a related topic to the book that you did enjoy. If nothing else, the same author tends to write in a similar style, and sometimes it is the style of writing and thinking that we relate to and appreciate, as much as the content itself.

Read related books

You can find related books that are recommended through Amazon or Goodreads to start. If you found a book to be beneficial, then seek out books similar to it. Otherwise, you may input other book titles into the search bar that you enjoyed in the past to find similar one to those.

Books recommended within the book you read

Often, a book you read will mention other interesting books within its pages, also there may be a list of references or a bibliography at the end, where it mentions books that the author used as source material. These are often a good start for learning more deeply about a topic, or for getting into related topics and themes.

Do not forget that you can see a list of *Recommended Readings* at the end of this book, which contains every book that has been mentioned in *The Insightful Reader* and additional useful recommendations.

Read something different

Go to a library or bookstore and wander around. I enjoy doing this because sometimes it feels best not to be constrained by a particular recommendation, and instead to be able to explore a variety of book shelves. If you have an idea of the genre you want to read, of course you can go to that section. Or if you are in the mood for something completely different, you can browse through genres that you may not normally read or give much attention to.

Check the book lists of people you admire

Recall that online, you can access the book recommendations of Bill Gates, Ryan Holiday, Oprah Winfrey, Reese Witherspoon, and other leaders (which were mentioned earlier in the book). Also remember that you can simply ask people who you admire which books they have enjoyed the most, and then you can read those. Even if you admire someone and you do not know him in person, you can search for his email address online and ask if he has any recommendations.

Concluding Thoughts

An Introduction

Now we will review some of the most important parts of *The Insightful Reader*, and some of the key ideas that will be important for you to remember and apply. There is some repetition here from earlier sections, but this is because some of these points are so important that I want to make sure you understand them.

Know Your WHY

Why are you doing anything? Why are you reading this book right now? Why do you read in general? Asking questions and knowing the purpose of your actions is critical. When you read, you have to know what you wish to get out of your reading, or you will likely come away with very little value in the end. This is one of the most common mistakes people make in both reading and in life.

Why are you on the path that you are on in life? What is it you are trying to accomplish? Is there an even better path you could be taking? Is there an even better way to accomplish what you want to accomplish? Why do you want to accomplish it in the first place? Clarifying the big *WHYs* of your life will often help give you great hints as to *WHAT* you should be reading.

When you choose what to read, some of the best starting points are to think about what area of your life you are bankrupt in, or in what area of your life you are the most motivated to make an improvement. Perhaps you want to learn more deeply about a topic such as psychology, but why? Are you trying to figure yourself out? Are you trying to understand other people? Or perhaps you want to read about physics, but why? Do you like math and how it can be applied? Do you want to understand the universe? When you want to know something, keep asking *WHY* to get to the deeper reasons. This will help you to learn more about yourself and will ultimately pay off more dividends. You must understand yourself, and then you can determine the best path for you to pursue. Of course, this is an ongoing journey, as it is difficult to know yourself fully – this takes time to accomplish. But we will not understand ourselves unless we ask ourselves questions and seek out the answers to them on a deeper level.

If you need some help figuring out why you choose to read, consider some of the following reasons:

- *Understand yourself* (e.g., your personality and feelings, your needs, how to improve yourself)
- *Understand other people* (e.g., why people do bad things, civilizations, governments, warfare)
- *Understand this planet* (e.g., global warming, natural life, geology)
- *Understand the universe* (e.g., physical rules, the origins of everything, the matter and energy that makes up the universe)
- *Solve a specific problem* (e.g., how to manage employees, how to invest your money, or alleviate the symptoms of a health condition)
- *Religious or spiritual reasons* (e.g., understand yourself, people, and the world through a religious or spiritual context)

If you are unsure of your WHY, keep reading and things will fall into place

Read *through* your problems, not just *because* you have a problem. There is a difference. I have chosen to read regularly, all the time, even when life is going great and I feel that I have things figured out. In these times I read more, not less. If you think this is strange, to read when there is no clear problem that needs solving, imagine a general responsible for defending his nation who does not see the use in training or learning during times of peace. Everything is going well, so what is the point in training and developing himself and his army? This is clearly short-sighted, and no one would want such a general to be responsible for defending their country. When war finally breaks out, do you want the general on your side who took a break during peace time, or the one who prepared for war during all of that time? Of course, you want the one who prepared. This is one of the reasons I choose to read even when everything in life is going great. You never know what you may learn during the good times that can help you during the bad times.

Similarly, I choose to read about how to deal with a wide range of problems all of the time. I am always in preparation to learn more and grow in my knowledge, understanding, and wisdom, so that when times are troubling, I have this reservoir of insights to fall back on. What motivates me further is knowing that if a loved one or someone I care about comes to me for advice, I will hopefully be able to provide some help, based on what I have learned. I find it very disturbing if someone asks me a question and I do not know the solution. In my deep learning, I have come to feel responsible for knowing how to solve problems that many people may not know how to approach. And if I cannot help someone immediately, often I will read and learn until I understand how the problem can be approached, hopefully to pursue a solution. A positive outcome of reading and learning regularly, is that after a period of time, *you become an expert in reading and learning, critical thinking, creative idea generation, and problem-solving.* Anything that you do not know, you will be able to figure out quite efficiently. This is a priceless skill to have.

Read and Think Adaptively

There is no one tip in this book that you need to follow all of the time. There are always exceptions. And this is something useful for you to remember, because some authors have a naturally authoritarian style where they tell you the facts or principles, and they do not always offer much of any room for flexibility. If a book is inflexible, you must find ways to think of the material and apply it in your life flexibly. As an example, if you are reading a book that tells you that you must purchase certain expensive software or equipment to accomplish your goals and you do not have the money, then you will need to figure out an alternative path to meet those goals. Perhaps you can find an equivalent cheaper software, or you can share the expensive software with a colleague.

You must adapt the book to meet your needs. A book is a static object that is not easily adaptable in a traditional sense – as naturally, words are static on a page. It is difficult for an author to write to all possible audiences and to all possible scenarios, and so you must think carefully about how you can apply the book to your particular case, or what a book's significance is to you. It is entirely possible that you will find some significance or meaning in the book that the author did not even intend – and that is fantastic. This means that you are truly doing your job as a diligent reader. You can read a book and attain your own unique insights from it – you do not always need to learn what the author intended to teach you.

When I was a child, one of my favorite book series was Choose Your Own Adventure. If you are unfamiliar with it, you would reach a certain point and the book would give you an option. *Turn to page 17 to confront the dragon or turn to page 73 to hide and hope you go unnoticed.* Then you would reach another key decision and have to make your choice, and you would actively participate in forming your own conclusion. I adored these as a child and I plowed through many of them, amazed at the adventures that I was able to create. It took me a long time to develop this insight, but in time I realized that **every book is a book where you choose the adventure.** You choose the type of book you want to read, you choose the book you will read, you choose how you want to read it (e.g., straight through, or skipping parts to maximize efficiency), you choose what the most important message of the book is, and you choose how you will apply it. At every step of the way you are making your own choices with a book and paving your own journey. Every book is a Choose Your Own Adventure book, in a sense.

Take Advantage of the Benefits of Reading

I already discussed many benefits to reading early in the book – such as that it is a highly effective and low cost way to learn, you can learn from the successes and failures of others, pursue your own education, improve your creativity and imagination, build up your empathy, expand your communication abilities, and discover who you truly are. These are immense, immense benefits. And when I hear about how little most people are reading, I am surprised at how much we seem to take all of this for granted. I believe a big part of our taking it for granted is that we get overwhelmed with there being too many books to read, *and* we feel that there is something better we could spend our time on. Most of us fear missing out on real life, and that is a valid point. However, we should remember that there are ***infinite insights*** in books that we could be missing out on as well. There is no reason to choose between books and life – they both synergize quite well together. I choose to read about an hour a day, and live life. I view this as quite a minor investment of my time, and I plan to read over a thousand insightful books in my lifetime with this simple habit.

If I had to sum up the benefits of reading, I would say that for all of human history, people have been trying to *figure things out.* Some of them have pursued religion or spiritual activities such as meditation, some pursued scientific progress, and others cultivated their artistic expression. And over the past thousand years or so, the vast majority of all books in existence have been created – where learned people have aimed to share their knowledge, wisdom, and understanding with us all. We are now in the perfect time to access ***all of this knowledge*** that has been recorded through books. I can communicate with renowned geniuses such as Albert Einstein, Leonardo da Vinci, and Isaac Newton through their books, or the books which have been written about them to learn what they knew. I may not communicate with their living forms, but I can communicate with their ideas, which never die. It is not easy of course to understand the insights that they acquired, but the knowledge is available for those who are willing to invest their time.

You do not need to do the hard work that other people have done to gain key insights. In many cases, people have been injured or killed in the pursuit of knowledge that is easily accessible through written symbols on a page that we all learn to recognize from a young age. *Words.* Remember that knowledge of what works and does not work on the battlefield has come at the cost of countless lives. Similarly, knowledge of what works and does not work in the medical field has come at the cost of countless lives. Also, knowledge about relationships or marriages has come at the cost of countless relationships – when the mistakes made were too great for them to recover, and people wrote books about those mistakes and how to prevent or overcome them. We see these words on a page and they seem like just words, but we should remember that **tremendous costs were paid so that we could learn about the better paths**. For every good path discovered, so many mistakes were made on the road to its discovery. It is easy to take for granted certain knowledge now that it has become a part of the social and cultural collective understanding, but the insights we now take for granted were unknown once upon a time. Books are one of the few products in existence, perhaps along with smart phones, computers, and the internet, where the value gained for the monetary cost is immense. It is hard to put a price on being able to access life-changing insights.

Use Your Newfound Reading Powers to Become an Expert Many Times Over

With a half hour of reading per day an average person may read 30 books in a year – of course it depends on your pace, reading skills, and the length and complexity of the books you read. If you read 30 books in a topic and you apply what you learn, you would likely be considered an expert by many people. Of course, your expertise will depend on the topic you read about. Some areas may be so specialist-oriented that 30 books would not be especially significant. For example, if you want to be a doctor, you will need a medical degree – no one will allow you to operate on him just because you read some books on the topic. Although in general, reading more books will go a long way toward helping you build expertise in a topic.

Now, I would like to present you with a strategy for building your expertise through reading.

First, acquire expertise in what truly interests you, what you are deeply motivated to learn more about. You can of course manage your life however you wish, but I admire the people who are willing to do what they believe in without focusing so much on the money behind it. If you become proficient at something, and you care about it enough to work harder than most of your competition, things often work out in the end for you. Also, even if you hold a steady job out of necessity, you can always build up your expertise in your true passion on the side. There is nothing stopping you from accomplishing what you want to do. Use books as a tool to help you get there.

You may of course seek to learn in areas that are more in demand or where people are earning more money, but economies boom and crash quite quickly these days. You may invest time and money to learn about something you are not interested in, hoping to make money, only later to find that the sector was overtaken by robots, or that the whole area went bankrupt, or that it became unnecessary because of other technological developments. It is your life and your option, but I do not recommend this path. Pursue something where you could still be happy even if you did not strike it rich.

I have built my expertise around psychology and self-development, writing, and business. A big chunk of my reading has been in these areas. I am also extremely interested in philosophy and this is something that I have been reading more about. The model I have used and that I recommend for building expertise is to become an expert in one thing, then the next, then the next. Focus on one thing at a time, or at least have one area dominate your focus at a time. I first became an expert in psychology when I gained my bachelor's degree at Purdue in 2007. Then, I pursued my master's degree in industrial-organizational psychology at the University of Oklahoma, where I furthered my expertise in psychology and was introduced to business concepts as well. However, I spent a lot of my time developing my writing skills while pursuing my degree, as this was important to my field and it was a weakness that I knew I wanted to strengthen. After graduating with my master's degree, I was comfortable with my expertise and skills in psychology and writing, but I felt rather weak in the area of business. Thus, I read many business books on my own time. Soon after this I started my own business as an author, where I implemented all three of my key expertise areas and put them into action – psychology, writing, and business. I think it helps greatly to choose areas of expertise that can be combined in some interesting way – as this is what I did. When you do this, you may find that you have little competition, especially if you focus on a combination of areas that most other people will not be skilled in. You are more than welcome to use this model for learning and building expertise if it helps you.

Keep in mind that expertise in *anything* can help you to build an understanding of other areas. When you learn one field deeply, it often becomes much easier to learn and make progress in other related fields. Focusing on related areas that synergize with each other in this way will present you with a highly efficient model for learning. Instead, if you learn deeply about areas that are not related, you may feel that you are being pulled in different directions, and you may be unsure of how to tie them together in a meaningful way. Of course, I always recommend learning widely, but when it comes to a career, it helps to have expertise in related areas that can support each other.

Also, consider learning in fields and areas that can be beneficial for many, many purposes. This may include some of the areas I have specialized in such as psychology, business, writing, and you may also include topics such as languages, art and design, public speaking and communication, general problem-solving skills, computer skills, and science and engineering. Many fields can be useful for different purposes, just consider what will be most important to learn for your life, in your situation, for your goals.

Stretch Your Reading Abilities

The way we get better at something is to stretch. If you never stretch your body, it will become very tight. But if you stretch, then the next day you will be slightly more flexible, and you can extend your muscles slightly more easily, then the next day you can stretch more, and you continue to become more flexible and mobile day by day. Using the same idea, stretch your reading by reading a few more pages today than you read yesterday. Or read something *slightly* more advanced or technical. Or read something in a new topic that challenges you, but not too much. These types of activities will make you stretch your reading abilities, and therefore help you to grow in your learning, reading, and thinking skills.

We are all capable of easily making gradual changes. If you do not have the habit of reading, start small. Start with reading five pages per day. When you start taking notes on your reading, do not necessarily jump into taking notes on everything discussed in this book. Just write down the insight you gained from what you read as a starting point. The point is to start somewhere. Do not put your reading aside for another day. *Start stretching your reading abilities right now.*

Experiment to Figure out What Works for You

I highly recommend experimenting to see what works best for you. In this book, I have included the best tips that have worked to help optimize my own reading habits. At certain points I have intuited the problems I thought you would have – and offered the best advice I could for overcoming such issues. Of course, I cannot intuit every possible problem you may have. Try the tips offered in *The Insightful Reader* – surely, some will work out better for you than others. Stick to the ones that pay off the most for you and avoid the ones that are not making much of a difference.

Have Fun

A key to making sure you keep reading will be to make sure you are enjoying it. Read books on topics that you truly want to learn about, not just ones that you feel you should learn about. It is important to do some reading that challenges and pushes you to a higher level – but something we can sometimes forget is that there should be some element of fun to it. Even if you decide you want to learn about a complex and challenging topic such as quantum physics, you should allow yourself to enjoy it. If the best way to enjoy it is to learn some principles through reading and then learn some through video tutorials of the material, that is perfectly fine. Or perhaps you would prefer to read a book on physics that has many jokes and funny illustrations. No problem. If reading seriously and for efficiency ruins the fun of it, then do not worry about that too much. I like to be as efficient with my reads as I can, but I also intermix fun with it. If I were reading to maximize my learning and understanding at all times, it may feel joyless and become counterproductive.

My parting words of advice: **Remember to have some fun with your reading and learning.**

Example Notes for The Insightful Reader

The following are example notes to give you an idea of how you may take notes for yourself when you read a book.

Title and Author

The Insightful Reader by I. C. Robledo

Goal

My goal with reading this book is to finally get into the habit of reading more books. I would like to read at least a book per month, and to learn how to pick better books to read, since I often feel that the book I chose was not a good fit for my needs.

Insights

- Read to gain insights, even if this requires more focus. This is better than reading many books passively without gaining much from them. The most valuable aspect of your readings will be the insights that you gain.
- Reading is perhaps the least costly and most effective way to learn. Out of all the options for learning, this is the best way for most people in most situations.
- Read books that will challenge you – such as books that are in fields unfamiliar to you, that are advanced, or from a perspective that you are generally unfamiliar with or opposed to. This is the path that will help you to make the most progress in your learning and understanding.
- After finishing a book and taking notes, evaluate your whole reading and note-taking process. Was there something you could have done better?

Key Points

- Ask many questions during my readings to make sure I have an active mind rather than a passive one.
- Investigate interesting books I may want to read carefully (title, cover, reviews, page count, sample, etc.), to see if they are truly worth reading.
- Take notes and review them periodically, for the books with key insights.
- Do not overlook the value of fiction – some of the greatest insights are hidden in between the lines of such books.
- I should always have many books available to me in many formats, to promote the habit of reading and make it easy for me to read, rather than putting up obstacles.
- Keep a list of the books I have read, the books I plan to read, and a separate list of the best and most insightful books I have read.
- This book has many insightful book recommendations at the end – check this list when I am not sure what book I would like to read next.

Quote

"Insights present you with a shift in the way you think about an idea or topic. They provide you with a realization that you should change the way you think about something and reconsider the actions that you take. Keep in mind that an insight for you is not necessarily an insight for someone else, or vice versa. Ultimately, an insight is personally meaningful to you."

Summary / Reflections

This has been a very practical book that will help me to read better books and gain more value from them. At every step of the reading process, even before the reading begins and after it ends, *The Insightful Reader* provides useful advice to gain important insights efficiently. This is a book I should take notes on and review those notes periodically to make sure I am on the right track with my reading goals.

Questions

- When I have no idea what to read next, how do I decide?
- How can I read more efficiently?
- If I am reading a book that is too difficult, what can I do?
- How many books should I be reading per year? What should I aim for?
- Is it fine to read multiple books at once?

Actions

- Record all the books I have read in Goodreads
- Record all of the books I would like to read in Goodreads
- Make a list of the best books I have read, and begin taking notes on those books gradually, so as not to overwhelm myself
- Begin taking notes on new books I read (using the tips in this book), focusing especially on any insights.
- Discuss this book with some friends or colleagues

Recommended Readings

This list of 200+ books includes all the books mentioned and recommended within *The Insightful Reader*. It also includes the most insightful books I have ever read (highlighted below), and the books I plan to read which I believe will be the most insightful. If you need help to figure out what to read next, this list will provide you with a starting point. For your enjoyment, I also included the two children's books mentioned earlier in the book.

LEARNING & MASTERY

How to Read a Book by Mortimer Adler and Charles Van Doren
Secrets of a Buccaneer Scholar by James Marcus Bach
***Make it Stick* by Peter C. Brown**
Moonwalking with Einstein by Joshua Foer
***Mastery* by Robert Greene**
***Self University* by Charles D. Hayes**
***Montessori* by Angeline Stoll Lillard**
The Secret Principles of Genius by I. C. Robledo
Effortless Reading by Vu Tran
***The Art of Learning* by Josh Waitzkin**
Merriam Webster's Vocabulary Builder

PSYCHOLOGY & SOCIOLOGY

Predictably Irrational by Dan Ariely
The Science of Love by John R. Baines
Six Thinking Hats by Edward de Bono
***Flow* by Mihaly Csikzentmihalyi**
***Mindset* by Carol S. Dweck**
The Hidden Order of Art by Anton Ehrenzweig
***Man's Search for Meaning* by Viktor Frankl**
Civilization and its Discontents by Sigmund Freud
Frames of Mind by Howard Gardner
Outliers by Malcolm Gladwell
***The 48 Laws of Power* by Robert Greene**

***On Killing* by Lt. Col. Dave Grossman**
The Righteous Mind by Jonathan Haidt
Healing and Recovery by David R. Hawkins
Transcending the Levels of Consciousness by David R. Hawkins
The Portable Jung by Carl Jung
Thinking, Fast and Slow by Daniel Kahneman
The Organized Mind by Daniel Levitin
***Thinking Allowed* by Jeffrey Mishlove**
From Depression to Contentment by Bob Rich
The Unthinkable by Amanda Ripley
***The 8 Laws of Change* by Stephan A. Schwartz**

PERSONAL DEVELOPMENT

***How to Fail at Almost Everything and Still Win Big* by Scott Adams**
Tuesday's with Morrie by Mitch Albom
Choose Yourself by James Altucher
***Reinvent Yourself* by James Altucher**
***How to Win Friends and Influence People* by Dale Carnegie**
***How to Stop Worrying and Start Living* by Dale Carnegie**
Atomic Habits by James Clear
***Daily Rituals* by Mason Currey**
The Miracle Morning by Hal Elrod
Tools for Titans by Timothy Ferriss
Stumbling on Happiness by Daniel Gilbert
***Mini Habits* by Stephen Guise**
The Book of Awakening by Mark Nepo
The War of Art by Steven Pressfield
Awaken the Giant Within by Anthony Robbins
365 Quotes to Live Your Life By by I. C. Robledo
***7 Thoughts to Live Your Life By* by I. C. Robledo**
***The Four Agreements* by Don Miguel Ruiz**
The Self-Sufficient Life and How to Live it by John Seymour
***The Top Five Regrets of the Dying* by Bronnie Ware**
The Wisdom of Sundays by Oprah Winfrey
SAS Survival Handbook by John Wiseman
The Seat of the Soul by Gary Zukav

BUSINESS & ENTREPRENEURSHIP

Getting Things Done by David Allen
Mistakes I Made at Work by Jessica Bacal
***Contagious* by Jonah Berger**
Business Adventures by John Brooks
***The Millionaire Fastlane* by M. J. DeMarco**
Measure What Matters by John E. Doerr
Business @ the Speed of Thought by Bill Gates
Checklist Manifesto by Atul Gawande
The Intelligent Investor by Benjamin Graham
The Hard Thing About Hard Things by Ben Horowitz
***The Personal MBA* by Josh Kaufman**
***15 Secrets Successful People Know About Time Management* by Kevin Kruse**
***Buy Buttons* by Nick Loper**
***Internet Business Insights* by Chris Naish**
***The 7 Levels of Change* by Rolf Smith**
The Black Swan by Nassim Nicholas Taleb
Zero to One by Peter Thiel
***#AskGaryVee* by Gary Vaynerchuk**
***Extreme Ownership* by Jocko Willink**
Lean Thinking by James Womack

BIOGRAPHIES

The Life and Times of Sonny Barger and the Hell's Angels Motorcycle Club by Sonny Barger
Shakespeare Saved My Life by Laura Bates
The Moth Presents All These Wonders by Catherine Burns
Bad Blood by John Carreyou
***Gifted Hands* by Ben Carson**
Titan by Ron Chernow
Don't Sleep, There Are Snakes by Daniel L. Everett
"Surely You're Joking, Mr. Feynman!" by Richard Feynman
***The Diary of a Young Girl* by Anne Frank**
***438 Days* by Jonathan Franklin**
The Moment of Lift by Melinda Gates
Einstein: His Life and Universe by Walter Isaacson
Leonardo da Vinci by Walter Isaacson

When Breath Becomes Air by Paul Kalanithi
The Story of My Life by Helen Keller
***Into the Wild* by Jon Krakauer**
Into Thin Air by Jon Krakauer
From Scratch by Tembi Locke
John von Neumann by Norman Macrae
Rosalind Franklin by Brenda Maddox
Long Walk to Freedom by Nelson Mandela
Born a Crime by Trevor Noah
Becoming by Michelle Obama
Bruce Lee by Matthew Polly
Just Kids by Patti Smith
Elon Musk by Ashlee Vance
Educated by Tara Westover
Whiskey in a Teacup by Reese Witherspoon
The Autobiography of Malcolm X by Malcolm X and Alex Haley
Autobiography of a Yogi by Paramahansa Yogananda
I am Malala by Malala Yousafzai

HISTORY & POLITICS

1001 Ideas that Changed the Way We Think by Robert Arp
The Library of Apollodorus by Apollodorus of Athens
Democracy and Dictatorship in Europe by Sheri Berman
***Big History* by Cynthia Stokes Brown**
The Rape of Nanking by Iris Chang
How the World Works by Noam Chomsky
The Second World War by Winston S. Churchill
Between the World and Me by Ta-Nehisi Coates
***Guns, Germs, & Steel* by Jared Diamond**
***The World Until Yesterday* by Jared Diamond**
An Indigenous Peoples' History of the United States by Roxanne Dunbar-Ortiz
Bad Days in History by Michael Farquhar
Harvest of Empire by Juan González
Mythology by Edith Hamilton
***Homo Deus* by Yuval Noah Harari**
Sapiens by Yuval Noah Harari
***The 100* by Michal H. Hart**

All Hell Let Loose by Max Hastings
Histories by Herodotus
Endurance by Alfred Lansing
Glimpses of World History by Jawaharlal Nehru
The Broken Ladder by Keith Payne
***A History of the World in 6 Glasses* by Tom Standage**
I Have a Dream by James Melvin Washington
The Professor and the Madman by Simon Winchester
The Post-American World by Fareed Zakaria
A People's History of the United States by Howard Zinn

PHILOSOPHY

***Meditations* by Marcus Aurelius**
***Utopia for Realists* by Rutger Bregman**
The Philosophy Book by Will Buckingham
50 Philosophy Classics by Tom Butler-Bowdon
The Hero with a Thousand Faces by Joseph Campbell
Understanding Power by Noam Chomsky
The Analects by Confucius
Logicomix by Apostolos Doxiadis
The Story of Philosophy by Will Durant
***The Art of Losing Control* by Jules Evans**
The Heart of the Buddha's Teaching by Thich Nhat Hanh
***Thank You for Arguing* by Jay Heinrichs**
The Obstacle is the Way by Ryan Holiday
A Treatise of Human Nature by David Hume
***A Guide to the Good Life* by William B. Irvine**
Brief Peeks Beyond by Bernardo Kastrup
Ramtha by J. Z. Knight
Insight by Bernard J. F. Lonergan
***The Prince* by Niccolo Machiavelli**
The Great Philosophers by Bryan Magee
The Shape of Ancient Thought by Thomas McEvilley
Food of the Gods by Terence McKenna
The Tibetan Book of the Dead by Padmasambhava
Enlightenment Now by Steven Pinker
The Republic by Plato
Letters from a Stoic by Seneca the Younger

Knowledge and Decisions by Thomas Sowell
Thoughts of a Philosophical Fighter Pilot by Jim Stockdale
***The Power of Now* by Eckhart Tolle**
Tao Te Ching by Lao Tzu
***The Art of War* by Sun Tzu**
A Little History of Philosophy by Nigel Warburton
Ten Things Video Games Can Teach Us by Jordan Erica Webber and Daniel Griliopoulos

SCIENCE & HEALTH

The Physics of Baseball by Robert Adair
The Science of Love by John R. Baines
The Unsettling of America by Wendell Berry
A Short History of Nearly Everything by Bill Bryson
The Systems View of Life by Fritjof Capra
The Tao of Physics by Fritjof Capra
The Epigenetics Revolution by Nessa Carey
***The Neurogenesis Diet and Lifestyle* by Brant Cortright**
Equations of Eternity by David Darling
Origins by Lewis Dartnell
The Origin of Species by Charles Darwin
Consciousness and the Brain by Stanislas Dehaene
Euclid's Elements by Euclid
Bad Science by Ben Goldacre
***How Not to Die* by Michael Greger and Gene Stone**
The Illustrated A Brief History of Time / The Universe in a Nutshell – Two Books in One by Stephen Hawking
On Intelligence by Jeff Hawkins
***The Sixth Extinction* by Elizabeth Kolbert**
The Structure of Scientific Revolutions by Thomas S. Kuhn
Brilliant Blunders by Mario Livio
***Cure* by Jo Marchant**
The Gene by Siddhartha Mukherjee
The Design of Everyday Things by Donald A. Norman
***In Defense of Food* by Michael Pollan**
The Demon-Haunted World by Carl Sagan
Behave by Robert M. Sapolsky
The Mathematical Theory of Communication by Claude Shannon

***Life 3.0* by Max Tegmar**
Black Holes & Time Warps by Kip S. Thorne
The Science of Interstellar by Kip S. Thorne
***Astrophysics for People in a Hurry* by Neil DeGrasse Tyson**
***Spontaneous Healing* by Andrew Weil**
The Uninhabitable Earth by David Wallace-Wells

LITERATURE

Arrow of God by Chinua Achebe
***The Alpha and the Omega* by Charley Ada**
The Hitchhiker's Guide to the Galaxy by Douglas Adams
Americanah by Chimamanda Ngozi Adichie
Aesop's Fables
The Power by Naomi Alderman
The Divine Comedy by Dante Alighieri
The Handmaid's Tale by Margaret Atwood
Emma by Jane Austen
God Speaks by Meher Baba
***The Stranger* by Albert Camus**
Alice's Adventures in Wonderland by Lewis Carroll
Don Quixote by Miguel de Cervantes
***The Alchemist* by Paulo Coelho**
The Brothers Karamazov by Fyodor Dostoyevsky
Notes from Underground, White Nights, the Dreams of a Ridiculous Man & Selections from the House of the Dead by Fyodor Dostoyevsky
The Complete Sherlock Holmes by Arthur Conan Doyle
Middlemarch by George Eliot
The Waste Land and Other Poems by T. S. Eliot
A Lesson Before Dying by Ernest J. Gaines
The Constant Princess by Philippa Gregory
Grimm's Fairy Tales by Jacob Grimm
The Cactus by Sarah Haywood
The Garden of Eden by Ernest Hemingway
Dune by Frank Herbert
***Hiroshima* by John Hersey**
Siddhartha by Hermann Hesse
The Illiad and *The Odyssey* by Homer
A Thousand Splendid Suns by Khaled Hosseini

Amerika by Franz Kafka
***One Flew Over the Cuckoo's Nest* by Ken Kesey**
***Flowers for Algernon* by Daniel Keyes**
Different Seasons by Stephen King
The Unbearable Lightness of Being by Milan Kundera
The Story of Dr. Dolittle by Hugh Lofting
***The Executioner's Song* by Norman Mailer**
The Magic Mountain by Thomas Mann
Moby-Dick by Herman Melville
The Song of Achilles by Madeline Miller
Watchmen by Alan Moore
The Bluest Eye by Toni Morrison
***1984* by George Orwell**
***Zen and the Art of Motorcycle Maintenance* by Robert M. Pirsig**
The Secrets We Kept by Lara Prescott
***In Search of Lost Time* by Marcel Proust**
***Ishmael* by Daniel Quinn**
Atlas Shrugged by Ayn Rand
Ascending Spiral by Bob Rich
The Little Prince by Antoine de Saint-Exupéry
***Blindness* by Jose Saramago**
The Complete Works of William Shakespeare
Star Maker by Olaf Stapledon
East of Eden by John Steinbeck
Wild by Cheryl Strayed
Perfume by Patrick Süskind
Gulliver's Travels by Jonathan Swift
The Lord of the Rings by J. R. R. Tolkien
War and Peace by Leo Tolstoy
Adventures of Huckleberry Finn by Mark Twain
The Pale King by David Foster Wallace
***Stoner* by John Williams**
Look Homeward, Angel by Thomas Wolfe
***The Shack* by William P. Young**

CHILDREN'S BOOKS

Choose Your Own Adventure series by R. A. Montgomery, Edward Packard, and other authors
Goosebumps series by R. L. Stine

Thank You

Thank you for taking the time to read *The Insightful Reader.* I hope that you found the information useful. Just remember that a key part of the learning process is putting what you read into practice.

Before you go, I want to invite you to pick up your free copy of *Step Up Your Learning: Free Tools to Learn Almost Anything.* All you have to do is type this link into your browser:

http://mentalmax.net/EN

Also, if you have any questions, comments, or feedback about this book, you can send me a message and I'll get back to you as soon as possible. Please put the title of the book you are commenting on in the subject line. My email address is:

ic.robledo@mentalmax.net

Did You Learn Something New?

If you found value in this book, please review it on Amazon so I can stay focused on writing more great books. Even a short one or two sentences would be helpful.

An Invitation to the "Master Your Mind" Community (on Facebook)

I founded a community where we can share advice or tips on our journey to mastering the mind. Whether you want to be a better learner, improve your creativity, get focused, or work on other such goals, this will be a place to find helpful information and a supportive network. I hope you join us and commit to taking your mind to a higher level.

To go directly to the page to join the community, you may type this into your web browser:

https://mentalmax.net/FB

More Books by I. C. Robledo

***365 Quotes to Live Your Life By* – FREE eBook!**

***7 Thoughts to Live Your Life By* – #1 Recommended Read**

The Intellectual Toolkit of Geniuses

Master Your Focus

The Smart Habit Guide

No One Ever Taught Me How to Learn

55 Smart Apps to Level Up Your Brain

Ready, Set, Change

Smart Life Book Bundle (Books 1-6)

The Secret Principles of Genius

Idea Hacks

Practical Memory

365 Quotes to Live Your Life By

7 Thoughts to Live Your Life By